A DISCIPLE'S

Journal

Daily Bible Reading and Guidance for Reflection

Year B
Revised Common Lectionary

Introduction by Steven W. Manskar

DISCIPLESHIP RESOURCES

PO BOX 340003 • NASHVILLE, TN 37203-0003

www.discipleshipresources.org

Cover design by Joey McNair, interior by Nanci Lamar

ISBN 0-88177-473-1
Library of Congress Control Number 2005929015

DR 473

CONTENTS

Introduction 6

Leading to the First Sunday of Advent 12
(Sunday between November 27 and December 3)

Leading to the Second Sunday of Advent 14
(Sunday between December 4 and 10)

Leading to the Third Sunday of Advent 16
(Sunday between December 11 and 17)

Leading to the Fourth Sunday of Advent 18
(Sunday between December 18 and 24)

The Days Surrounding Christmas 20
(December 19 through December 25)

The Days Surrounding Christmas 22
(December 26 through December 31)

The Days Surrounding Christmas 24
(January 1 through January 6)

Leading to the Baptism of the Lord 26
(Sunday between January 7 and 13)

Leading to the Second Sunday after the Epiphany 28
(Sunday between January 14 and 20)

Leading to the Third Sunday after the Epiphany 30
(Sunday between January 21 and 27)
If this is the last Sunday after Epiphany, use the week leading to Transfiguration Sunday.

Leading to the Fourth Sunday after the Epiphany 32
(Sunday between January 28 and February 3)
If this is the last Sunday after Epiphany, use the week leading to Transfiguration Sunday.

Leading to the Fifth Sunday after the Epiphany 34
(Sunday between February 4 and 10)
If this is the last Sunday after Epiphany, use the week leading to Transfiguration Sunday.

Leading to the Sixth Sunday after the Epiphany 36
(Sunday between February 11 and 17)
If this is the last Sunday after Epiphany, use the week leading to Transfiguration Sunday.

Leading to the Seventh Sunday after the Epiphany 38
(Sunday between February 18 and 24)
If this is the last Sunday after Epiphany, use the week leading to Transfiguration Sunday.

CONTENTS

Leading to the Eighth Sunday after the Epiphany 40
(Sunday between February 25 and 29)

Leading to Transfiguration Sunday 42
(Last Sunday after the Epiphany)

Leading to Ash Wednesday and the First Sunday in Lent 44

Leading to the Second Sunday in Lent 46

Leading to the Third Sunday in Lent 48

Leading to the Fourth Sunday in Lent 50

Leading to the Fifth Sunday in Lent 52

Leading to Palm/Passion Sunday 54

Holy Week 56

Leading to the Second Sunday of Easter 58

Leading to the Third Sunday of Easter 60

Leading to the Fourth Sunday of Easter 62

Leading to the Fifth Sunday of Easter 64

Leading to the Sixth Sunday of Easter 66

Leading to the Seventh Sunday of Easter 68

Leading to the Day of Pentecost 70

Leading to Trinity Sunday 72

Leading to Sunday between May 24 and 28 74
(If after Trinity Sunday)

Leading to Sunday between May 29 and June 4 76
(If after Trinity Sunday)

Leading to Sunday between June 5 and 11 78
(If after Trinity Sunday)

Leading to Sunday between June 12 and 18 80
(If after Trinity Sunday)

Leading to Sunday between June 19 and 25 82
(If after Trinity Sunday)

CONTENTS

Leading to Sunday between June 26 and July 2 84

Leading to Sunday between July 3 and 9 86

Leading to Sunday between July 10 and 16 88

Leading to Sunday between July 17 and 23 90

Leading to Sunday between July 24 and 30 92

Leading to Sunday between July 31 and August 6 94

Leading to Sunday between August 7 and 13 96

Leading to Sunday between August 15 and 20 98

Leading to Sunday between August 21 and 27 100

Leading to Sunday between August 28 and September 3 102

Leading to Sunday between September 4 and 10 104

Leading to Sunday between September 11 and 17 106

Leading to Sunday between September 18 and 24 108

Leading to Sunday between September 25 and October 1 110

Leading to Sunday between October 2 and 8 112

Leading to Sunday between October 9 and 15 114

Leading to Sunday between October 16 and 22 116

Leading to Sunday between October 23 and 29 118

Leading to Sunday between October 30 and November 5 120

Leading to Sunday between November 6 and 12 122

Leading to Sunday between November 13 and 19 124

Leading to Christ the King / Reign of Christ 126
    (Sunday between November 20 and 26)

An Order of Devotion 128

INTRODUCTION

"O that we may all receive of Christ's fullness, grace upon grace;
grace to pardon our sins, and subdue our iniquities;
to justify our persons and to sanctify our souls;
and to complete that holy change, that renewal of our hearts,
whereby we may be transformed
into that blessed image wherein thou didst create us."
John Wesley

From "A Collection of Forms of Prayer for Every Day of The Week"

A *Disciple's Journal* is a guide for witnessing to Jesus Christ in the world and for following his teachings, under the guidance of the Holy Spirit, through acts of compassion, justice, worship, and devotion. God makes the "holy change" (as John Wesley prays above) real when we participate in and cooperate with the grace freely given to the world through works of piety (prayer, worship, the Lord's Supper, Bible study, fasting or abstinence) and works of mercy (feeding the hungry, welcoming strangers, clothing the naked, caring for the sick, and visiting prisoners). This *Journal* will help you attend to practicing these basics of Christian discipleship, known as the means of grace. These are the places God has promised to meet us, and through which God will form your character into the character of Christ.

A Disciple's Journal is structured to help you maintain balance in your discipleship between the works of piety (loving God through acts of worship and devotion with all your heart, soul, mind and strength), and the works of mercy (loving your neighbor as yourself through acts of justice and compassion).

There are two pages for each week. The left-hand page is a guide for daily devotion (Bible reading, hymn singing, and prayer). Space is provided to record prayers, prayer concerns, praise, and questions that arise during the week.

A brief excerpt from *The Works of John Wesley* is included each week. These are provided as a source of reflection and learning about the Wesleyan/Methodist tradition. These excerpts will peak

your curiosity and move you to read the sermons and other writings of John and Charles Wesley. They have much to say to us today. The excerpts contained in the *Journal, Year B* are all taken from "A Plain Account of Christian Perfection" found in *The Works of John Wesley,* edited by Thomas Jackson.

The right-hand page is the journal. Space is provided for you to record what you have done to grow in loving God and loving your neighbor each week. This page is divided into four quadrants, each corresponding to loving God (acts of worship and acts of devotion) and loving neighbors (acts of justice and acts of compassion).

On page 128 you will find guides for daily morning and evening prayer. They are taken from *The Book of Common Prayer.* They are simple, adaptable, and grounded in the church's tradition. As you make them part of your daily practice of prayer, you will find that each day will be wrapped in the Word of God contained in Holy Scripture and, if you include hymns, canticles, and the creed, the communion of saints will walk with you.

A Daily Lectionary

A Disciple's Journal contains a daily lectionary that is intended to support and supplement the Revised Common Lectionary (RCL). What is a lectionary? It is a systematic way of reading through the Bible guided by the Church's liturgical calendar (beginning the first Sunday of Advent through the feast of Christ the King, near the end of November). It helps the Church read, pray, and celebrate God's actions in history through the people of Israel, in the life, ministry, death, and resurrection of Jesus Christ, and through the life and witness of the early Church. Four Scripture lessons are selected for each week; two lessons from the Old Testament (one from the historical, wisdom, or prophetic books and a Psalm) and two lessons from the New Testament (verses from an Epistle and one of the Gospels). The Revised Common Lectionary is divided into a three-year cycle (A, B, and C). Each year emphasizes one of the Synoptic Gospels (A: Matthew, B: Mark, C: Luke) with significant portions of the Gospel According to John included in each year. Because the RCL is intended for use in worship, it necessarily neglects significant portions of the Bible. The daily lectionary included with the *Journal* is intended to fill in the gaps in the RCL.

Hoyt Hickman developed the daily lectionary found in *A Disciple's Journal* for the Order of St. Luke. *The Daily Lectionary: A Guide for Using the Scriptures Within the Daily Office* is available from Order of St. Luke Publications, PO Box 22279, Akron, OH 44302-0079. It is used here by permission.

The Psalm

You will see that there is a Psalm, or Psalm portion, assigned for each week. Because the Psalms is the prayer book of the Bible, we recommend that you read the Psalm each day of the week.

Read it slowly, like a prayer, and let it sink into your soul, heart, and mind. You may want to memorize it by the end of the week so that it will stay with you always. Another way of engaging the Psalms is to chant them. Chanting is a way of singing the Psalms. It is how the Church has engaged these Scripture songs and prayers from its very beginning. If you wish to explore this historic practice, look at pages 736-737 of *The United Methodist Hymnal*. All of the Psalms contained in the Psalter are "pointed" in order to facilitate chanting. You will also find five different chant tones. Most of the Psalms used in the Revised Common Lectionary may be found in the Psalter of *The United Methodist Hymnal*.

THE HYMN

A hymn is selected for each week. Hymns are an important resource for faith formation, inspiration, and theological reflection in the Wesleyan/Methodist tradition. All of the hymns are found in *The United Methodist Hymnal*. Like the Psalm, it is recommended that the hymn for the week be either said or sung each day. Take time to reflect upon the words and allow them to sink into your soul, heart, and mind. Let them become part of you. You may want to memorize them along with the Psalm.

DAILY SCRIPTURE LESSONS

Two Scripture lessons are provided for each day of the week. Most days' lessons are taken from both the Old and New Testaments. They include the lessons assigned for the week by the Revised Common Lectionary, along with passages around them. You may want to read one of the lessons in the morning and the other in the evening. Read slowly and meditatively. Savor the words. Pay attention to the words and phrases that jump off the page for you so they may guide your prayers. Remember, you are reading not for information but for God's Word to form you, fill you, and prepare you for prayer.

PRAYER FOR OURSELVES AND FOR OTHERS

"And first, all who desire the grace of God are to wait for it in the way of prayer. This is the express direction of our Lord himself. In his Sermon upon the Mount, after explaining at large wherein religion consists, and describing the main branches of it, he adds: 'Ask, and it shall be given you; seek, and ye shall find; knock, and it shall be opened unto you. For everyone that asketh, receiveth; and he that seeketh, findeth; and to him that knocketh, it shall be opened.' (Matthew 7:7, 8) Here we are in the plainest manner directed to ask in order to, or as a means of, receiving; to seek in order to find the grace of God, the pearl of great price (Matthew 13:46); and to knock, to continue asking and

seeking, if we would enter into his kingdom" (John Wesley, Sermon 16: The Means of Grace, §III.1).

We see from the quote above that John Wesley believed prayer is the "chief means" by which God conveys grace to us. Prayer is simply spending time with God. It is sharing with God your needs and hopes for yourself, those whom you love, and the world. Prayer is honest communication with the Beloved. You also need to allow time to listen for God and attend to God's movement with, in, and through you.

THE LORD'S PRAYER

The Lord's Prayer is yet another way the Church connects us to God. It is a summary of Christian faith. Some have said that Christians are people who pray this prayer. Jesus gave this prayer to his disciples as a way of teaching them how to pray as he prays. In it he helps us remember who and whose we are. This prayer is an expression of our shared faith in the living God who became one of us in Jesus Christ.

THE COLLECT

The daily orders for morning and evening prayer each conclude with a collect in the back of the *Journal*. This is an ancient form of prayer with roots that go back to the early church. A Collect generally has five parts: address, attribution/ascription, petition, purpose, and closing. These prayers help us focus on the attributes and person of God—on God's goodness, faithfulness and justice. They are an excellent way of learning and teaching others to pray. A Collect for each day of the week, morning and evening, is provided on the back flap of the *Journal*. You may also use this flap to bookmark your journey through the year. The Collects included here are taken from *The Book of Common Prayer*.

THE JOURNAL

The facing page is divided into four quadrants designed for recording the acts of compassion, justice, worship, and devotion you have done during the week. The purpose of this page is to help you strive toward a balanced life of discipleship that is centered in Christ and guided by the General Rule of Discipleship: "To witness to Jesus Christ in the world, and to follow his teachings through acts of compassion, justice, worship, and devotion under the guidance of the Holy Spirit." This General Rule is a guide, grounded in the Wesleyan/Methodist tradition, intended to help Christians make sure they attend to all the teachings of Jesus and not only those that suit individual temperaments. Jesus summarized his teachings in Matthew 22:37-39, "'You shall love the Lord your God with all your heart, and all your soul, and all your mind.' This is the greatest and first commandment. And a second is like it: 'You shall love your neighbor as yourself.' On these two commandments hang all the law and the prophets."

Through acts of worship and devotion, God has given us the means to grow in our love for God. Through acts of compassion and justice, God has given us the means to live out our love of God by loving those whom God loves, as God loves them. John Wesley called these "the means of grace . . . outward signs, words, or actions ordained of God, and appointed for this end, to be the ordinary channels whereby he might convey to men preventing, justifying, or sanctifying grace" (John Wesley, Sermon 16: The Means of Grace, §II.1). They include:

- Acts of Compassion—the simple things we do out of kindness for our neighbor. Your neighbor is anyone who is in need, anywhere in the world.
- Acts of Justice—we must not only minister to people in need, but also ask why they are in need. In the name of Christ, we must implement God's righteousness and denounce injustice.
- Acts of Worship—the means of grace that we exercise together; the ministries of word and sacrament. They enable us to build each other up in the Body of Christ.
- Acts of Devotion—the private spiritual disciplines of prayer, Bible reading, and inward examination that bring us face to face with God.

COVENANT DISCIPLESHIP GROUPS

Covenant Discipleship groups are a contemporary adaptation of the early Methodist class meeting. A group is five to seven persons who meet together for one hour each week to hold themselves mutually accountable for their discipleship. They do this by means of a covenant they have written, shaped by the General Rule of Discipleship.

Members of Covenant Discipleship groups "watch over one another in love" by giving each other a weekly compass heading. The task-oriented gatherings give members the opportunity to help each other become better disciples. It is a trustworthy and effective way of identifying and nurturing leaders in discipleship for mission and ministry. Covenant Discipleship groups are not where our discipleship happens, but where we make sure that it happens.

A Disciple's Journal was developed especially for Covenant Discipleship groups as a means of helping group members attend to their covenant between weekly meetings. Group members should bring their journal to the meeting to guide them as they share with the group what they have done, and not done in their daily walk with Christ in the world. The *Journal* will also help guide daily Bible reading, prayer, and provide a place to record prayer concerns shared by other group members.

To learn more about Covenant Discipleship groups, visit the web site at http://www.gbod.org/smallgroup/cd. You may also write or call the Director of Accountable Discipleship at The General Board of Discipleship at 877-899-2780; PO Box 340003, Nashville, TN 37203-0003; smanskar@gbod.org.

Help us to help each other, Lord,
Each other's cross to bear;
Let each his friendly aid afford,
And feel his brother's care.
Help us to build each other up,
Our little stock improve;
Increase our faith, confirm our hope,
And perfect us in love.

Charles Wesley

A Collection of Hymns for Use for the Use of The People Called Methodists, #489:3-4.

Psalm: 80:1-7, 17-19

Hymn: "O Come and Dwell in Me" (UMH 388)

Monday
Isaiah 64:1-9
1 Corinthians 1:3-9

Tuesday
Mark 13:24-37
Isaiah 2:1-5

Wednesday
Romans 13:11-14
Matthew 24:36-44

Thursday
1 Thessalonians 3:9-13
Luke 21:25-36

Friday
Deuteronomy 30:11-14
Romans 10:8b-18

Saturday
Matthew 4:18-22
John 1:35-42

Sunday
Mark 13:24-37
Jeremiah 33:14-16

PRAYER Concerns

A Word from John Wesley

In the year 1729 I began not only to read but to study the Bible, as the one, the only standard of truth, and the only model of pure religion. Hence I saw, in a clearer and clearer light, the indispensable necessity of having the mind which was in Christ, and of walking as Christ also walked; even of having not some part only, but all the mind which was in Him; and of walking as He walked, not only in many or in most respects, but in all things. And this was the light wherein, at this time, I generally considered religion, as a uniform following of Christ, an entire inward and outward conformity to our Master.

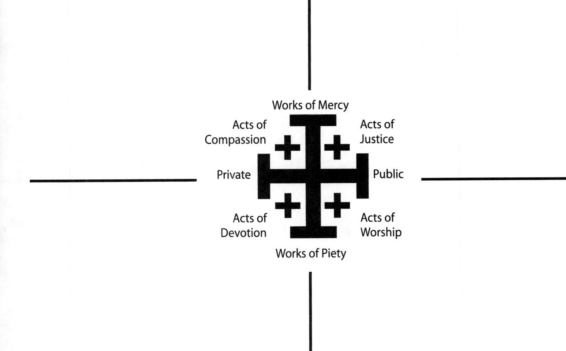

Works of Mercy

Acts of
Compassion

Acts of
Justice

Private

Public

Acts of
Devotion

Acts of
Worship

Works of Piety

To witness to Jesus Christ in the world and to follow his teachings
through acts of compassion, justice, worship, and devotion under the guidance of the Holy Spirit.

LEADING TO THE SECOND SUNDAY OF ADVENT

(Sunday between December 4 and 10)

Psalm 85:1-2, 8-13

Hymn: "Prepare the Way of the Lord" (UMH 207)

Monday
Isaiah 40:1-11
2 Peter 3:8-15a

Tuesday
Mark 1:1-8
Isaiah 11;1-10

Wednesday
Romans 15:4-13
Matthew 3:1-12

Thursday
Malachi 3:1-4
Philippians 1:3-11

Friday
Luke 3:1-6
Baruch 5:1-9

Saturday
Isaiah 40:1-11
2 Peter 3:8-15a

Sunday
Mark 1:1-8
1 Thessalonians 5:16-24

Prayer Concerns

A Word from John Wesley

"Love is the fulfilling of the law, the end of the commandment." It is not only the first and great command, but all the commandments in one: "Whatever things are just, whatever things are pure, if there be any virtue, if there be any praise," they are all comprised in this one word, LOVE. In this is perfection, and glory, and happiness! The royal law of heaven and earth is this, "You shall love the Lord your God with all your heart, and with all your soul, and with all your mind, and with all your strength." The one perfect good shall be your one ultimate end.

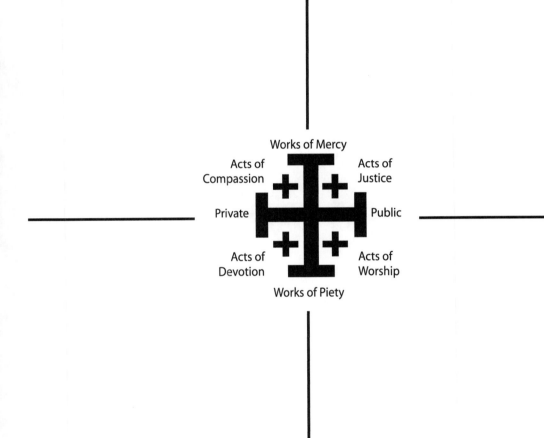

To witness to Jesus Christ in the world and to follow his teachings
through acts of compassion, justice, worship, and devotion under the guidance of the Holy Spirit.

LEADING TO THE THIRD SUNDAY OF ADVENT
(Sunday between December 11 and 17)

Psalm 126

Hymn: "Of the Father's Love Begotten" (UMH 184)

Monday
Isaiah 61:1-4, 8-11
John 1:6-8, 19-28

Tuesday
Isaiah 35:1-10
Matthew 11:2-15

Wednesday
Malachi 4:1-6
Matthew 17:10-13

Thursday
James 5: 7-10
Zephaniah 3:14-20

Friday
Philippians 4:4-9
Luke 3:7-20

Saturday
Isaiah 61:1-4, 8-11
1 Thessalonians 5:16-24

Sunday
John 1:6-8, 19-28
Romans 16:25-27

PRAYER Concerns

A Word from John Wesley

Desire not to live but to praise His name; let all your thoughts, words, and works tend to His glory. Let your soul be filled with so entire a love to Him, that you may love nothing but for His sake. Have a pure intention of heart, a steadfast regard to His glory in all your actions. For then, and not till then, is that mind in us which was also in Christ Jesus, when in every motion of our heart, in every word of our tongue, in every work of our hands, we pursue nothing but in relation to Him, and in subordination to His pleasure; when . . . "whether we eat or drink, or whatever we do, we do it all to the glory of God."

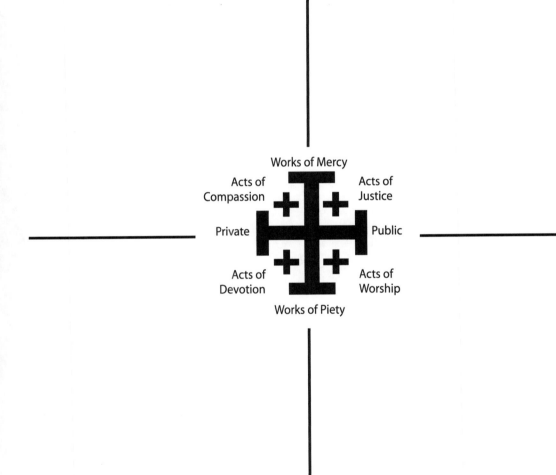

Works of Mercy

Acts of Compassion

Acts of Justice

Private

Public

Acts of Devotion

Acts of Worship

Works of Piety

To witness to Jesus Christ in the world and to follow his teachings
through acts of compassion, justice, worship, and devotion under the guidance of the Holy Spirit.

LEADING TO THE FOURTH SUNDAY OF ADVENT
(Sunday between December 18 and 24)

Psalm: Luke 1:47-55

Hymn: "O Come, O Come, Emmanuel" (UMH 211)

Monday
2 Samuel 7:1-11, 16
Luke 1:26-38

Tuesday
Romans 1:1-7
Matthew 1:1-17

Wednesday
Isaiah 7:10-16
Matthew 1:18-25

Thursday
Micah 5:2-5a
Hebrews 10:4-10

Friday
Zechariah 9:9-10
John 3:16-21

Saturday
Jeremiah 23:5-6
Luke 3:23-38

Sunday
Haggai 2:6-9
Revelation 12:1-5

PRAYER Concerns

A Word from John Wesley

If you are a Methodist . . . you love the Lord your God with all your heart, with your soul, with all your mind, and with all your strength. God is the joy of your heart, and the desire of your soul, which is continually crying, "Whom have I in heaven but Thee? And there is none upon earth whom I desire besides Thee." My God and my all! "Thou art my strength of my heart, and my portion for ever."

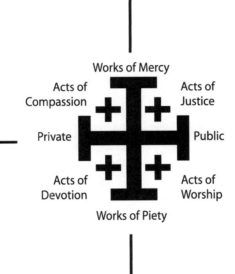

Works of Mercy

Acts of
Compassion

Acts of
Justice

Private

Public

Acts of
Devotion

Acts of
Worship

Works of Piety

To witness to Jesus Christ in the world and to follow his teachings
through acts of compassion, justice, worship, and devotion under the guidance of the Holy Spirit.

THE DAYS SURROUNDING CHRISTMAS
(December 19 through December 25)

Hymn: "Hark! the Herald Angels Sing" (UMH 240)

PRAYER Concerns

December 19
Isaiah 9:2-7; Psalm 96
Titus 2:11-14

December 20
Luke 1:1-17; Psalm 113
Luke 1:18-25

December 21
Hebrews 10:35–11:1; Psalm 126
John 20:24-29

December 22
Luke 1:26-33; Psalm 40:1-11
Luke 1:34-38

December 23
1 Samuel 2:1-10; Luke 1:47-55
Luke 1:39-45, 56

December 24
Luke 1:57-80
Luke 2:1-20; Psalm 96

December 25 (Christmas Day)
Isaiah 52:7-10; Psalm 98
Hebrews 1:1-12; John 1:1-18

A Word from John Wesley

And loving God, [a Methodist] "loves your neighbor as yourself"; you love everyone as your own soul. You love your enemies; yea, and the enemies of God. And if it be not your power to "do good to them that hate you," yet you cease not to "pray for them," though they spurn your love, and still "despitefully use you, and persecute you."

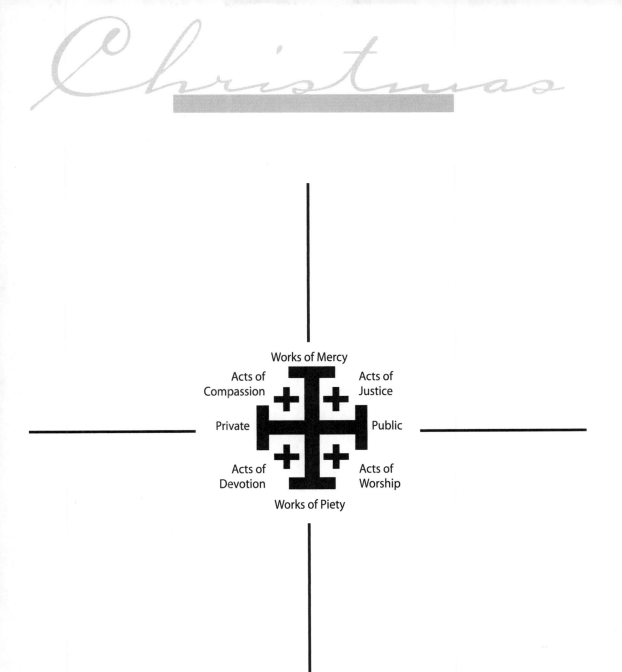

Works of Mercy

Acts of Compassion   Acts of Justice

Private   Public

Acts of Devotion   Acts of Worship

Works of Piety

To witness to Jesus Christ in the world and to follow his teachings
through acts of compassion, justice, worship, and devotion under the guidance of the Holy Spirit.

Hymn: "Joy to the Word" (UMH 246)

December 26
Acts 6:1–7:2a, 51-60; Psalm 31
Matthew 23:34-39

December 27
1 John 1:1-9; Psalm 92
John 21:19b-24

December 28
Jeremiah 31:15-17; Psalm 124
Matthew 2:13-33

December 29
Isaiah 63:7-9; Psalm 148
Hebrews 2:10-18

December 30
Ecclesiastes 3:1-13; Psalm 8
Numbers 6:22-27

December 31
Revelation 21:1-6a
Philippians 2:5-11

PRAYER Concerns

A Word from John Wesley

O Savior of all who trust in You, do with me what seems best in Your own eyes, only give me the mind of Christ. Let me learn from You how to be meek and humble, pouring into me the spirit of humility. Fill, I ask You most fervently, every part of my soul, and make Your Spirit the constant, ruling habit of my mind. Make all emotions rise from Your Spirit. I want no thoughts, no desires, no designs, but what come truly from You . . .

From A Collection of *Forms of Prayer for Every Day in the Week.*

Works of Mercy

Acts of
Compassion

Acts of
Justice

Private

Public

Acts of
Devotion

Acts of
Worship

Works of Piety

To witness to Jesus Christ in the world and to follow his teachings
through acts of compassion, justice, worship, and devotion under the guidance of the Holy Spirit.

THE DAYS SURROUNDING CHRISTMAS
(January 1 through January 6)

Hymn: "Christ, Whose Glory Fills the Skies" (UMH 173)

January 1
Matthew 25:31-46
Luke 2:15-21

January 2
Isaiah 60:1-6;
Psalm 72:1-7, 10-14
Ephesians 3:1-12

January 3
Jeremiah 31:7-14
Matthew 2:1-12

January 4
Ephesians 1:3-14
John 1:10-18

January 5
Isaiah 60:1-6
Ephesians 3:1-12

January 6
(The Epiphany of the Lord)
Matthew 2:1-12
Isaiah 49:1-6

PRAYER Concerns

A Word from John Wesley

Fix my heart on Jesus with ardent love so I will respond to the inspiration that comes from such love, and resolve to follow Him in all paths of humble, meek and patient living. Help me run with patience the race, looking to Jesus, Author and Finisher of my faith.

So preserve me that I will not despise or faint under your corrections, and even if I go through terrible troubles, make me nonetheless in complete subjection to You and to live in the hope of eternal glory. More, make me rejoice, even glory, in tribulations, for Christ's sake. Amen.

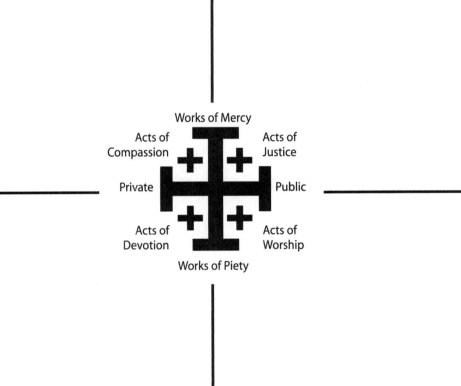

Works of Mercy

Acts of Compassion

Acts of Justice

Private

Public

Acts of Devotion

Acts of Worship

Works of Piety

To witness to Jesus Christ in the world and to follow his teachings
through acts of compassion, justice, worship, and devotion under the guidance of the Holy Spirit.

Psalm 29

Hymn: "Come, Let Us Use the Grace Divine" (UMH 606)

Monday
Genesis 1:1-5
Acts 19:1-7

Tuesday
Mark 1:4-11
Isaiah 43:1-7

Wednesday
Acts 8:14-17
Luke 3:15-17, 21-22

Thursday
Isaiah 42:1-9
Acts 10:34-43

Friday
Matthew 3:13-17
Acts 2:37-39

Saturday
Genesis 1:1-5
Acts 19:1-7

Sunday
Mark 1:4-11
Isaiah 42:10-25

PRAYER Concerns

A Word from John Wesley

For as [a Methodist] loves God, "so you keep His commandments": not only some, or most of them, but ALL, from the least to the greatest. You are not content to "keep the whole law, and offend in one point," but have, in all points, "a conscience void of offense, towards God, and towards man." Whatever God has forbidden, you avoid; whatever God has enjoined, you do. "You run the way of God's commandments," now He hath set your heart at liberty. It is your glory and joy so to do: it is your daily crown of rejoicing, to do the will of God on earth as it is done in heaven.

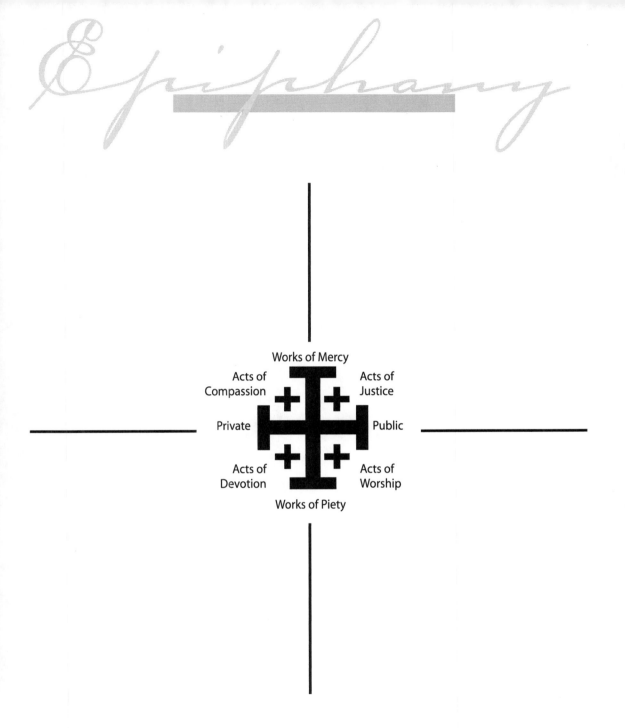

To witness to Jesus Christ in the world and to follow his teachings
through acts of compassion, justice, worship, and devotion under the guidance of the Holy Spirit.

Psalm 139:1-6, 13-18

Monday
 1 Samuel 1:1-18
 John 1:35-42

Tuesday
 1 Samuel 1:19-28
 John 1:43-51

Wednesday
 1 Samuel 2:1-10
 1 Corinthians 4:14-21

Thursday
 1 Samuel 2:11-21
 1 Corinthians 5

Friday
 1 Samuel 2:22-36
 1Corinthians 6:1-8

Saturday
 1 Samuel 3
 1 Corinthians 6:9-11

Sunday
 1 Corinthians 6:12-20
 John 2:1-11

Hymn: "O, For a Heart to Praise My God" (UMH 417)

PRAYER Concerns

A Word from John Wesley

Nor do the customs of the world at all hinder [a Methodist] "running the race which is set before you." You cannot, therefore, "lay up treasures upon earth," no more than you can take fire into your bosom. You cannot speak evil of your neighbor, any more than you can lie either to God or man. You cannot utter any unkind word of anyone; for love keeps the door of your lips. … But "whatever things are pure, whatever things are lovely, whatever things are" justly "of good report," you think, speak, and act, "adorning the doctrine of God our Savior in all things."

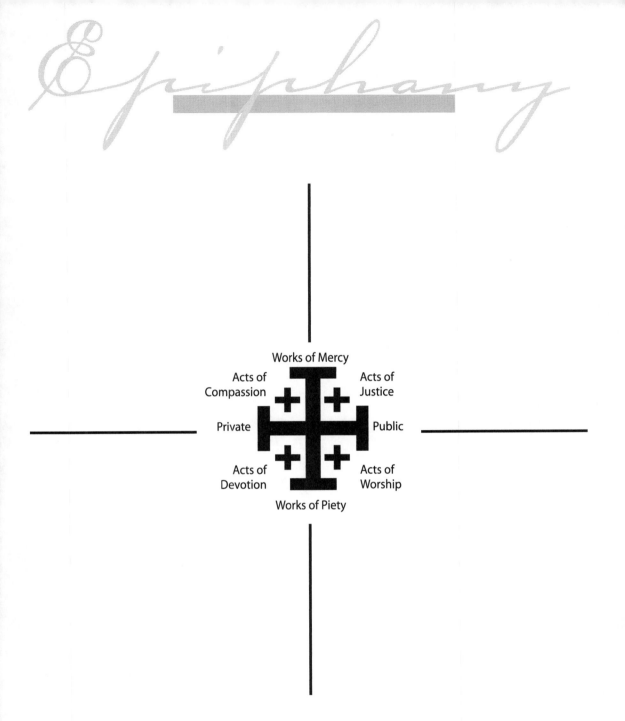

Works of Mercy

Acts of Compassion

Acts of Justice

Private

Public

Acts of Devotion

Acts of Worship

Works of Piety

To witness to Jesus Christ in the world and to follow his teachings
through acts of compassion, justice, worship, and devotion under the guidance of the Holy Spirit.

Psalm 62:5-12

Monday
Jonah 1:1-10
Mark 1:14-20

Tuesday
Jonah 1:11-17
1 Corinthians 7:1-7

Wednesday
Jonah 2
1 Corinthians 7: 8-16

Thursday
Jonah 3
1 Corinthians 7:17-24

Friday
Jonah 4:1-5
1 Corinthians 7:25-35

Saturday
Jonah 4:6-11
1 Corinthians 7:36-40

Sunday
Mark 1:14-20
Deuteronomy 9:6-29

Hymn: "Lord of the Dance" (UMH 261)

PRAYER Concerns

A Word from John Wesley

He, therefore, who lives in these Christians, has purified their hearts; insomuch that every one that has Christ in them, "the hope of glory, purifies himself even as He is pure." He is purified from pride; for Christ was lowly in heart. He is pure from desire and self-will, for Christ desired only to do the will of His Father. And He is pure from anger, in the common sense of the word; for Christ was meek and gentle. I say, in the common sense of the word; for He is angry at sin while He is grieved for the sinner. He feels anger at every offense against God, but only tender compassion to the offender.

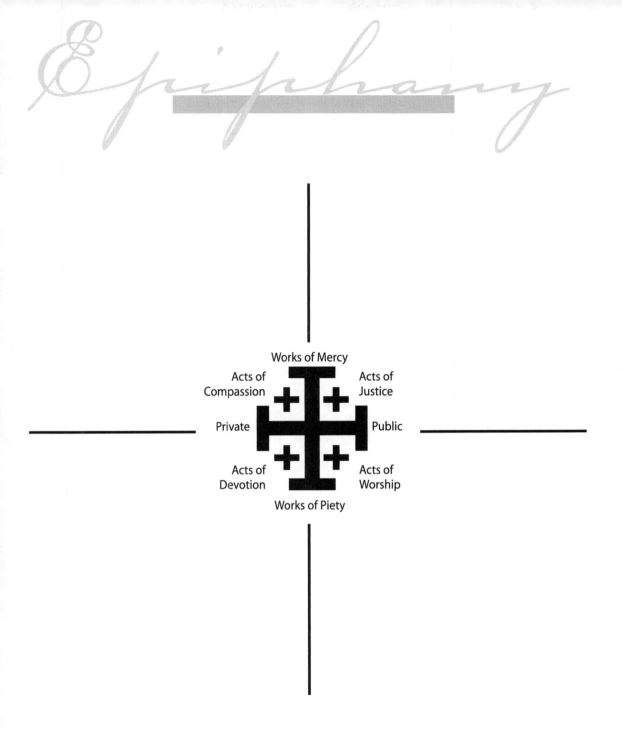

Works of Mercy

Acts of
Compassion

Acts of
Justice

Private

Public

Acts of
Devotion

Acts of
Worship

Works of Piety

To witness to Jesus Christ in the world and to follow his teachings
through acts of compassion, justice, worship, and devotion under the guidance of the Holy Spirit.

Psalm 111

Hymn: "Christ Whose Glory Fills the Skies" (UMH 173)

Monday
Deuteronomy 10:1-11
Mark 1:21-28

Tuesday
Deuteronomy 10:12-22
1 Corinthians 8

Wednesday
Deuteronomy 11:18-21
Deuteronomy 12:15-24

Thursday
Deuteronomy 14:22-29
Deuteronomy 15:1-11

Friday
Deuteronomy 15:12-18
Deuteronomy 16:18-20

Saturday
Deuteronomy 18:1-8
Deuteronomy 18:15-20

Sunday
Mark 1:21-28
Deuteronomy 19

PRAYER Concerns

*If this is the last Sunday after Epiphany, use the week leading to Transfiguration Sunday.

A Word from John Wesley

This great gift of God, the salvation of our souls, is no other than the image of God fresh stamped on our hearts. It is the "renewal of believers in the spirit of their minds, after the likeness of Him that created them." God has now laid "the axe unto the root of the tree," "purifying their hearts by faith," and "cleansing all the thoughts of their hearts by the inspiration of His Holy Spirit."

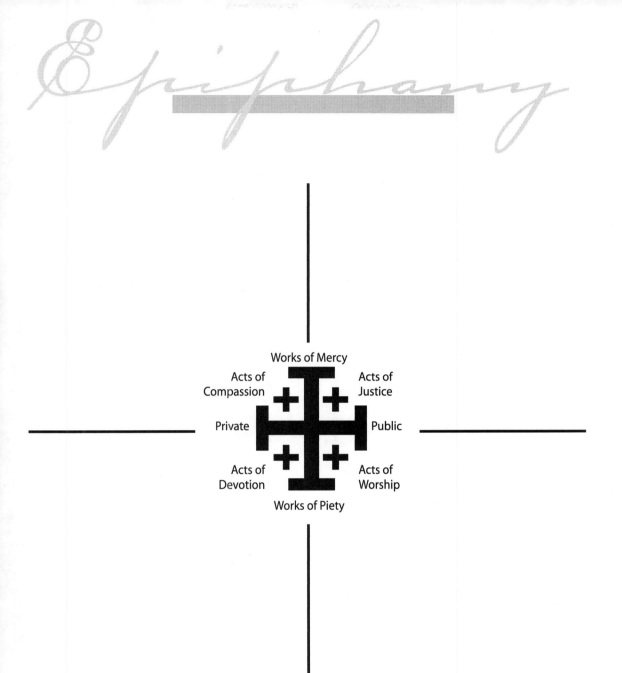

To witness to Jesus Christ in the world and to follow his teachings
through acts of compassion, justice, worship, and devotion under the guidance of the Holy Spirit.

LEADING TO THE FIFTH SUNDAY AFTER THE EPIPHANY
(Sunday between February 4 and 10)*

Psalm 147

Hymn: "O For a Thousand Tongues to Sing" (UMH 57)

Monday
Isaiah 40:1-11
Mark 1:29-34

Tuesday
Isaiah 40:12-27
Mark 1:35-39

Wednesday
Isaiah 40:28-31
1 Corinthians 9:1-14

Thursday
Isaiah 41:1-13
1 Corinthians 9:16-23

Friday
Isaiah 41:17-20
Isaiah 42:1-4

Saturday
Isaiah 42:5-17
Isaiah 42:18-25

Sunday
Mark 1:29-39
2 Kings 4:38-44

PRAYER Concerns

*If this is the last Sunday after Epiphany, use the week leading to Transfiguration Sunday.

A Word from John Wesley

And "where the Spirit of the Lord is, there is liberty;" such liberty "from the law of sin and death" as the children of this world will not believe, though a man declare it unto them. "The Son hath made them free," who are thus "born of God," from that great root of sin and bitterness, pride. They feel that all their "sufficiency is of God"; that it is He alone who "is in all their thoughts," and "worketh in them both to will and to do of His good pleasure." They feel that "it is not they" that "speak, but the Spirit of" their "Father who speaketh in them"; and that whatsoever is done by their hands, "the Father, who is in them, He doeth the works."

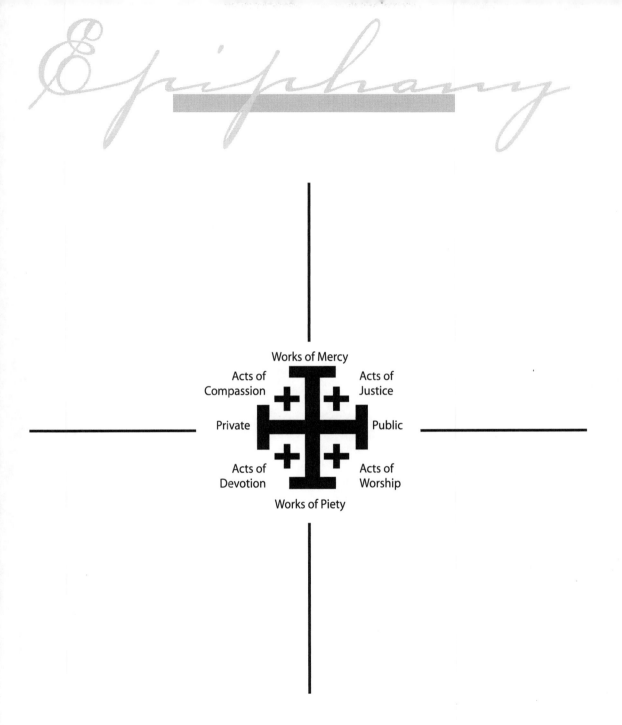

Works of Mercy

Acts of
Compassion

Acts of
Justice

Private

Public

Acts of
Devotion

Acts of
Worship

Works of Piety

To witness to Jesus Christ in the world and to follow his teachings
through acts of compassion, justice, worship, and devotion under the guidance of the Holy Spirit.

LEADING TO THE SIXTH SUNDAY AFTER THE EPIPHANY
(Sunday between February 11 and 17*)

Psalm 30

Hymn: "Hear Us, Emmanuel, Hear Our Prayer"
(UMH 266)

Monday
    2 Kings 5:1-14
    Mark 1:40-45

Tuesday
    2 Kings 5:15-19
    1 Corinthians 9:24-27

Wednesday
    2 Kings 5:20-27
    1 Corinthians 10:1-13

Thursday
    1 Corinthians 10:14-22
    1 Corinthians 10:23–11:1

Friday
    1 Corinthians 11:2-16
    1 Corinthians 11:17-34

Saturday
    1 Corinthians 12:1-11
    1 Corinthians 12:12-26

Sunday
    1 Corinthians 13
    1 Corinthians 14:1-19

PRAYER Concerns

If this is the last Sunday after Epiphany, use the week leading to Transfiguration Sunday.

A Word from John Wesley

Indeed, how God may work, we cannot tell; but the general manner wherin He does work is this: Those who once trusted in themselves that they were righteous that they were rich, and increased in goods, and had need of nothing, are, by the Spirit of God applying His word, convinced that they are poor and naked. All the things that they have done are brought to their remembrance, and set in array before them; so that they see the wrath of God hanging over their heads, and feel that they deserve the damnation of hell. In their trouble they cry out unto the Lord, and He shows them that He hath taken away their sins, and opens the kingdom of heaven in their hearts, "righteousness, and peace, and joy in the Holy Ghost."

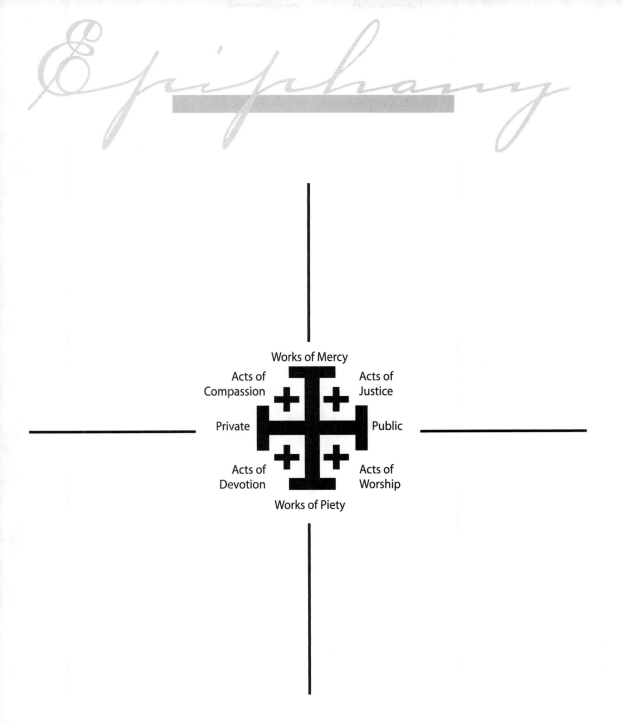

Works of Mercy

Acts of Compassion

Acts of Justice

Private

Public

Acts of Devotion

Acts of Worship

Works of Piety

To witness to Jesus Christ in the world and to follow his teachings
through acts of compassion, justice, worship, and devotion under the guidance of the Holy Spirit.

Leading to the Seventh Sunday after the Epiphany

(Sunday between February 18 and 24*)

Psalm 41

Monday
Isaiah 43:1-7
1 Corinthians 14:20-40

Tuesday
Isaiah 43:8-13
Mark 2:1-12

Wednesday
Isaiah 43:14-25
1 Corinthians 15:1-28

Thursday
Isaiah 43:26–44:8
1 Corinthians 15:29-58

Friday
Isaiah 44:9-23
1 Corinthians 16

Saturday
Isaiah 44:24–45:13
2 Corinthians 1:1-11

Sunday
2 Corinthians 1:12-22
2 Corinthians 1:23–2:13

*If this is the last Sunday after Epiphany, use the week leading to Transfiguration Sunday.

Hymn: "Come, Ye Sinners, Poor and Needy" (UMH 340)

Prayer Concerns

A Word from John Wesley

From every evil motion freed
(The Son hath made us free)
On all the powers of hell we tread,
In glorious liberty.

Come, Father, Son, and Holy Ghost,
And seal me Thine abode!
Let all I am in Thee be lost;
Let all be lost in God.

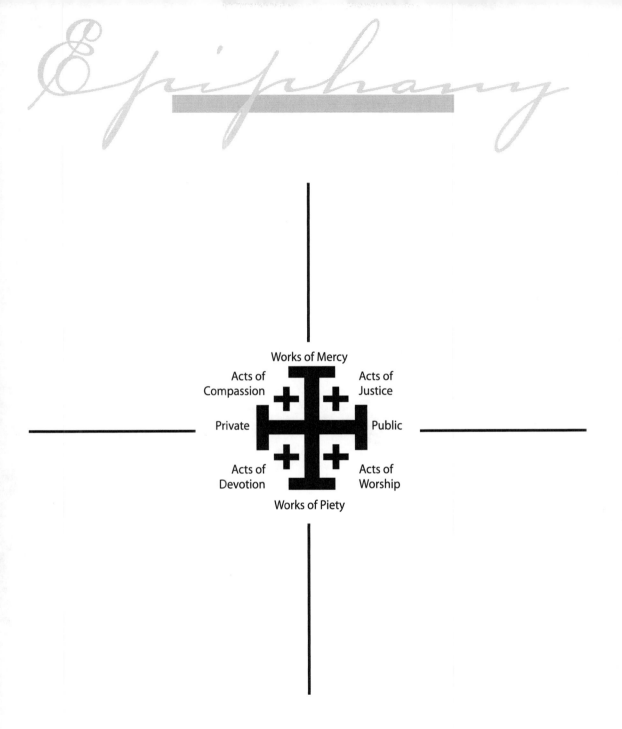

Works of Mercy

Acts of
Compassion

Acts of
Justice

Private

Public

Acts of
Devotion

Acts of
Worship

Works of Piety

To witness to Jesus Christ in the world and to follow his teachings
through acts of compassion, justice, worship, and devotion under the guidance of the Holy Spirit.

LEADING TO THE EIGHTH SUNDAY AFTER THE EPIPHANY
(Sunday between February 25 and 29)

Psalm 103

Hymn: "Sois la Semilla (You Are the Seed)" (UMH 583)

Monday
Hosea 2:14-20
Mark 2:13-17

Tuesday
2 Corinthians 2:14–3:6
Mark 2:18-20

Wednesday
Mark 2:21-22
Mark 2:23-28

Thursday
Mark 3:1-6
Mark 3:7-12

Friday
Mark 3:13-19
Mark 3:19b-30

Saturday
Mark 3:31-35
Mark 4:1-20

Sunday
Mark 4:21-25
Mark 4:26-34

PRAYER Concerns

If this is the last Sunday after Epiphany, use the week leading to Transfiguration Sunday.

A Word from John Wesley

Perhaps the general prejudice against Christian perfection may chiefly arise from the misapprehension of the nature of it. We willingly allow, and continually declare, there is no such perfection in this life as implies either a dispensation from doing good, and attending all the ordinances of God; or a freedom from ignorance, mistake, temptation, and a thousand infirmities necessarily connected with flesh and blood.

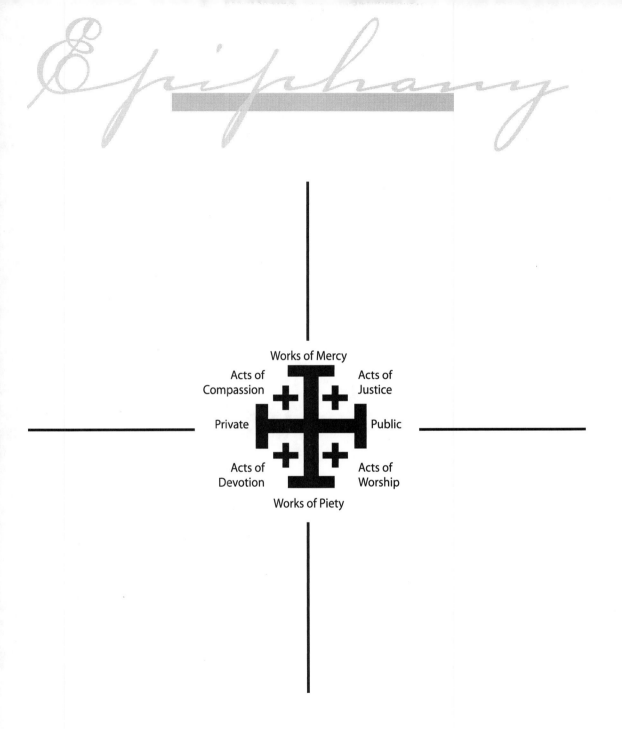

To witness to Jesus Christ in the world and to follow his teachings
through acts of compassion, justice, worship, and devotion under the guidance of the Holy Spirit.

Psalm 50:1-6

Hymn: "Christ, Whose Glory Fills the Skies" (UMH 173)

Monday
2 Kings 2:1-12
2 Kings 2:13-15

Tuesday
Mark 9:2-13
Mark 9:14-29

Wednesday
Exodus 34:29-35
2 Corinthians 3:7-11

Thursday
Exodus 24:12-18
2 Corinthians 3:12–4:2

Friday
2 Corinthians 4:3-6
Luke 9:28-43

Saturday
2 Peter 1:16-21
Matthew 17:1-9

Sunday
Mark 9:2-9
Mark 9:14-29

PRAYER Concerns

A Word from John Wesley

First, we not only allow, but earnestly contend, that there is no perfection in this life which implies any dispensation from attending all the ordinances of God; or from doing good unto all men while we have time, though "especially unto the household of faith." We believe that not only babes in Christ, who have newly found redemption in His blood, but those also who are "grown up into perfect men," are indispensably obliged, as often as they have opportunity, to "eat bread and drink wine in remembrance of Him," . . .

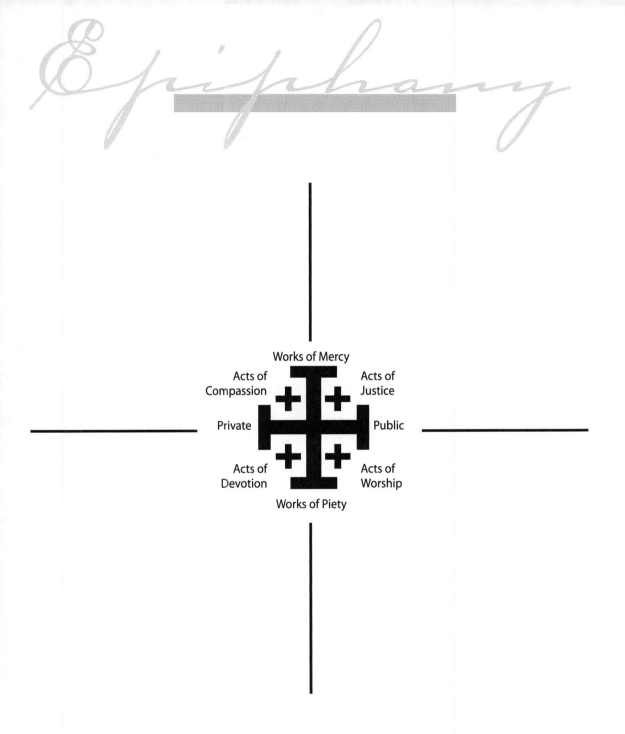

Works of Mercy

Acts of
Compassion

Acts of
Justice

Private

Public

Acts of
Devotion

Acts of
Worship

Works of Piety

To witness to Jesus Christ in the world and to follow his teachings
through acts of compassion, justice, worship, and devotion under the guidance of the Holy Spirit.

Leading to Ash Wednesday:
Leading to the First Sunday in Lent:

Monday
   Joel 2:1-2, 12-17
   Matthew 6:1-6

Tuesday
   2 Corinthians 5:20b-21
   Matthew 6:16-21

Wednesday
   2 Corinthians 6:1-2
   2 Corinthians 6:3-10

Thursday
   Genesis 6:11-22
   1 Peter 3:18-22

Friday
   Genesis 9:1-17
   Mark 1:1-15

Saturday
   Genesis 2:15-17
   Romans 5:1-19

Sunday
   Genesis 3:1-7
   Romans 3:19-26

Psalm 51:1-7
Psalm 25:1-10
Hymn: "Lord, Who Throughout These Forty Days"
(UMH 269)

PRAYER Concerns

A Word from John Wesley

We, secondly, believe that there is no such perfection in this life as implies an entire deliverance either from ignorance or mistake, in things not essential to salvation, or from manifold temptations, or from numberless infirmities, wherewith the corruptible body more or less presses down the soul. We cannot find any ground in Scripture to suppose that any inhabitant of a house of clay is wholly exempt either from bodily infirmities, or from ignorance of many things; or to imagine any is incapable of mistake, or falling into diverse temptations.

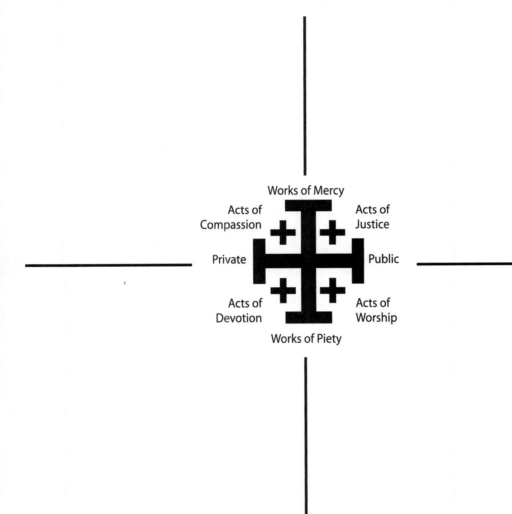

Works of Mercy

Acts of Compassion

Acts of Justice

Private

Public

Acts of Devotion

Acts of Worship

Works of Piety

To witness to Jesus Christ in the world and to follow his teachings
through acts of compassion, justice, worship, and devotion under the guidance of the Holy Spirit.

Psalm 22:23-31

Hymn: "Take Up Thy Cross" (UMH 415)

Monday
Genesis 12:1-9
Mark 8:31-38

Tuesday
Genesis 15:1-6
Romans 4:1-5

Wednesday
Genesis 15:7-21
Romans 4:6-12

Thursday
Genesis 17:1-7
Romans 4:13-25

Friday
Genesis 17:15-22
John 3:1-8

Saturday
Philippians 3:17–4:1
John 5:19-24

Sunday
Mark 8:31-38
Exodus 19:1-8

PRAYER *Concerns*

A Word from John Wesley

But whom then do you mean by "one that is *perfect*." We mean one in "whom is the mind which was in Christ," and who so "walketh as Christ also walked"; a man "that hath clean hands and a pure heart," or that is "cleansed from all filthiness of flesh and spirit": one in whom is "no occasion of stumbling," and who accordingly "does not commit sin." … We understand hereby, one whom God hath "sanctified throughout, in body, soul, and spirit"; one who "walketh in the light as He is in the light; in whom is no darkness at all: the blood of Jesus Christ His Son having cleansed him from all sin."

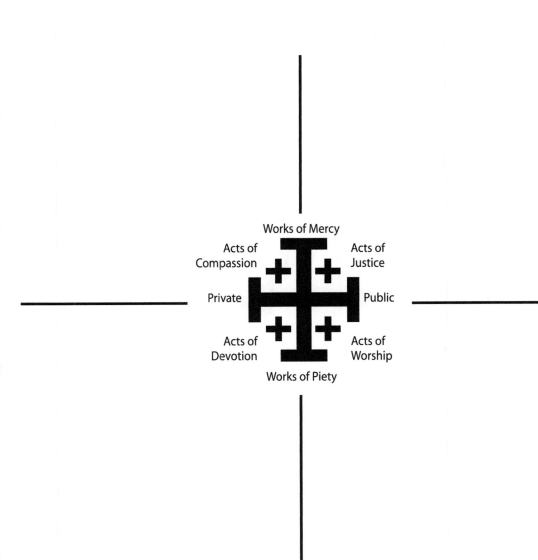

Works of Mercy

Acts of
Compassion

Acts of
Justice

Private

Public

Acts of
Devotion

Acts of
Worship

Works of Piety

To witness to Jesus Christ in the world and to follow his teachings
through acts of compassion, justice, worship, and devotion under the guidance of the Holy Spirit.

Psalm 19

Hymn: "O Young and Fearless Prophet" (UMH 444)

Monday
Exodus 20:1-6
John 2:13-22

Tuesday
Exodus 20:7-11
1 Corinthians 1:10-17

Wednesday
Exodus 20:12
1 Corinthians 1:18-25

Thursday
Exodus 20:13-14
1 Corinthians 1:26-31

Friday
Exodus 20:15-16
John 4:5-26

Saturday
Exodus 20:17
John 4:27-42

Sunday
John 2:13-22
Ephesians 1:15-23

Prayer Concerns

A Word from John Wesley

This man can now testify to all mankind, "I am crucified with Christ: nevertheless I live; yet not I, but Christ lives in me." He is "holy as God who called him is holy," both in heart and "in all manner of conversation." He "loves the Lord his God with all his heart," and serves Him with "all his strength." He "loves his neighbor," every one, "as himself"; "yea," as Christ "loves us"; them in particular that "despitefully use him, and persecute him, because they know not the Son, neither the Father." Indeed his soul is all love; filled with "compassion, kindness, meekness, gentleness, patience."

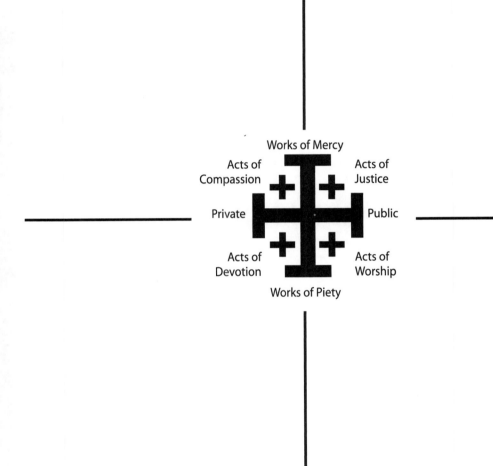

Works of Mercy

Acts of
Compassion

Acts of
Justice

Private

Public

Acts of
Devotion

Acts of
Worship

Works of Piety

To witness to Jesus Christ in the world and to follow his teachings
through acts of compassion, justice, worship, and devotion under the guidance of the Holy Spirit.

Psalm 108:1-3, 17-22

Monday
Numbers 21:4-9
John 3:14-21

Tuesday
Ephesians 2:1-7
Ephesians 2:8-10

Wednesday
1 Samuel 16:1-13
John 9:1-17

Thursday
Ephesians 5:8-14
John 9:18-41

Friday
2 Corinthians 5:16-21
Luke 15:1-7

Saturday
Luke 15:8-10
Luke 15:11-32

Sunday
John 3:14-21
John 11:1-16

Hymn: "O Love Divine, What Hast Thou Done?"
(UMH 287)

A Word from John Wesley

This it is to be a perfect man, to be "sanctified throughout"; even "to have a heart so all-flaming with the love of God" . . . "as continually to offer up every thought, word, and work, as a spiritual sacrifice, acceptable to God, through Christ"; in every thought of our hearts, in every word of our tongues, in every work of our hands, to "show forth His praise, who hath called us out of darkness into His marvelous light." Oh that both we, and all who seek the Lord Jesus is sincerity, may thus be made perfect in one!

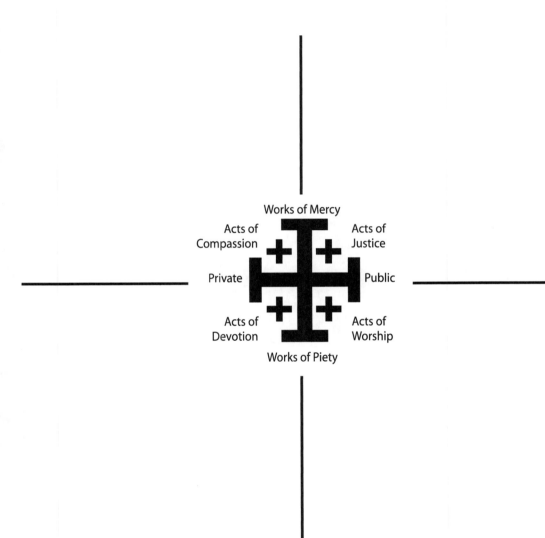

Works of Mercy

Acts of
Compassion

Acts of
Justice

Private

Public

Acts of
Devotion

Acts of
Worship

Works of Piety

To witness to Jesus Christ in the world and to follow his teachings
through acts of compassion, justice, worship, and devotion under the guidance of the Holy Spirit.

Psalm 51:1-12

Monday
Ezekiel 37:1-14
John 11:17-27

Tuesday
Hebrews 5:1-10
John 11:28-45

Wednesday
Jeremiah 31:31-34
John 12:1-8

Thursday
Isaiah 43:16-21
John 12:20-26

Friday
Philippians 3:4b-11
John 12:27-33

Saturday
Philippians 3:12-14
Romans 8:6-11

Sunday
Romans 8:12-17
Philippians 2:5-11

Hymn: "Ask Ye What Great Thing I Know" (UMH 163)

PRAYER Concerns

A Word from John Wesley

Our first conception of [Christian perfection] was, It is to have 'the mind which was in Christ,' and to 'walk as He walked'; to have all the mind that was in Him, and always to walk as He walked: in other words, to be inwardly and outwardly devoted to God; all devoted in heart and life.

Lent

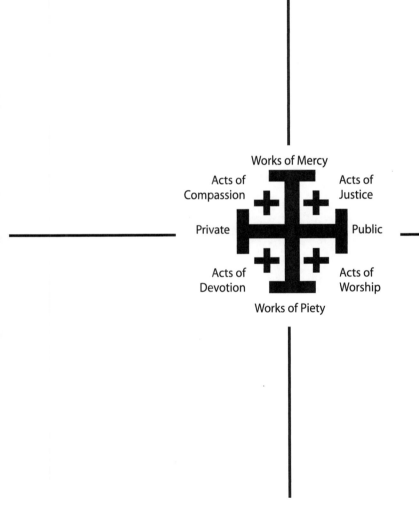

Works of Mercy

Acts of
Compassion

Acts of
Justice

Private

Public

Acts of
Devotion

Acts of
Worship

Works of Piety

To witness to Jesus Christ in the world and to follow his teachings
through acts of compassion, justice, worship, and devotion under the guidance of the Holy Spirit.

Hymn: "Ye Servants of God" (UMH 181)

Monday
Mark 11:1-11
Mark 11:12-33
Psalm 118:1-2, 19-29

Tuesday
Isaiah 50:4-9a
Philippians 2:5-11
Psalm 31:9-16

Wednesday
Mark 14:1-11
Mark 14:12-25

Thursday
Mark 14:26-42
Mark 14:43-52

Friday
Mark 14:53-72
Mark 15:1-15

Saturday
Mark 15:16-24
Mark 15:25-39

Sunday
Mark 15:40-47
John 12:12-19

PRAYER Concerns

A Word from John Wesley

Savior from sin, I wait to prove
That Jesus is Thy Healing name;
To lose, when perfected in love,
Wate'er I have, or can, or am:
I stay me on they faithful word,
"The servant shall be as his Lord."

Didst Thou not die, that I might live
No longer to myself, but Thee?
Might body, soul, and spirit give
To Him who gave Himself for me?
Come then, my Master, and my God,
Take the dear purchase of Thy blood.

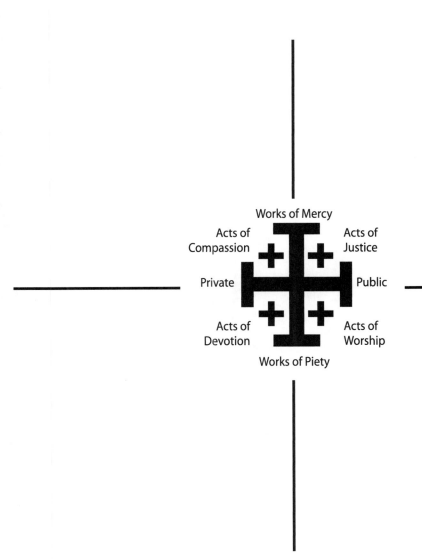

To witness to Jesus Christ in the world and to follow his teachings
through acts of compassion, justice, worship, and devotion under the guidance of the Holy Spirit.

Monday
Isaiah 42:1-9; Psalm 36:5-11
Hebrews 9:11-15; John 12:1-11

Tuesday
Isaiah 49:1-7; Psalm 71:1-14
1 Corinthians 1:18-31;
John 12:20-36

Wednesday
Isaiah 50:4-9a; Psalm 70
Hebrews 12:1-3; John 13:21-32

Thursday
Exodus 12:1-14;
Psalm 116:1-4, 12-19
1 Corinthians 11:23-26;
John 13:1-17, 31b-35

Friday
Isaiah 52:13–53:12, Psalm 22
Hebrews 10:16-25;
John 18:1–19:42

Saturday
Genesis 2:1-3; Psalm 130
Romans 6:3-11; Mark 16:1-8

Sunday (Easter)
Acts 10:34-43;
Psalm 118:1-2, 14-24
1 Corinthians 15:1-11;
John 20:1-18

Hymns: "O Love Divine, What Hast Thou Done?" (UMH 287)
"Come, Sinners, to the Gospel Feast" (UMH 616)

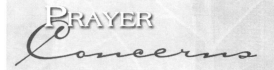

PRAYER Concerns

A Word from John Wesley

Now let me gain perfection's height!
Now let me into nothing fall,
Be less than nothing in my sight,
And feel that Christ is all in all!

Lord, I believe Thy work of grace
Is perfect in the soul!
His heart is pure who sees Thy face,
His spirit is made whole.

From every sickness, by Thy word,
From every foul disease,
Saved, and to perfect health restored,
To perfect holiness.

He walks in glorious liberty,
To sin entirely dead;
The Truth, the Son, hath made him free,
And he is free indeed.

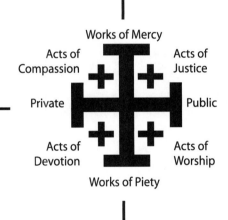

Works of Mercy

Acts of
Compassion

Acts of
Justice

Private

Public

Acts of
Devotion

Acts of
Worship

Works of Piety

To witness to Jesus Christ in the world and to follow his teachings
through acts of compassion, justice, worship, and devotion under the guidance of the Holy Spirit.

Psalm 133

Hymn: "Love Divine, All Loves Excelling" (UMH 384)

Monday
Acts 2:14a, 22-32
Matthew 28:9-15

Tuesday
Acts 4:32-35
John 20:19-23

Wednesday
Acts 4:36–5:11
John 20:24-31

Thursday
1 John 1-4
John 21:1-14

Friday
1 John 1:5–2:2
John 21:15-19

Saturday
Isaiah 26:2-9, 19
John 21:20-25

Sunday
John 20:19-31
Acts 3:1-11

PRAYER Concerns

A Word from John Wesley

On Monday, June 25, 1744, our first conference began …. The next morning we seriously considered the doctrine of sanctification, or perfection. The questions asked concerning it, and the substance of the answers given, were as follows:

Q: What is it to be *sanctified*?

A: To be renewed in the image of God, *in righteousness and true holiness.*

Q: What is implied in being a *perfect Christian*?

A: The loving God with all our heart, and mind, and soul (Deuteronomy. 6:5).

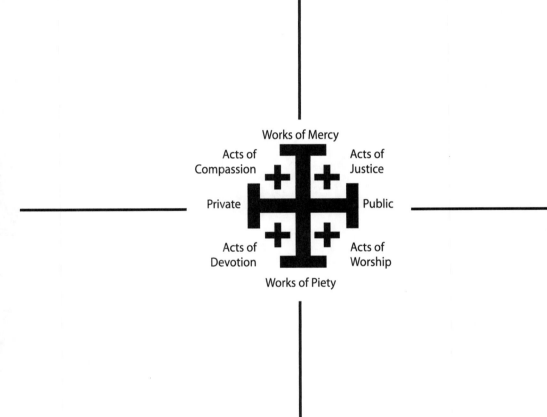

Works of Mercy

Acts of Compassion

Acts of Justice

Private

Public

Acts of Devotion

Acts of Worship

Works of Piety

To witness to Jesus Christ in the world and to follow his teachings
through acts of compassion, justice, worship, and devotion under the guidance of the Holy Spirit.

Psalm 4

Monday
Acts 3:12-16
Luke 24:1-12

Tuesday
Acts 3:17-26
Luke 24:13-35

Wednesday
1 John 3:1-3
Luke 24:36-43

Thursday
1 John 3:4-10
Luke 24:44-53

Friday
Micah 4:1-5
1 Peter 1:1-9

Saturday
1 Peter 1:10-16
1 Peter 1:17-25

Sunday
Luke 24:36b-48
1 John 3:11-15

Hymn: "He Is Lord" (UMH 177)

PRAYER
Concerns

A Word from John Wesley

Our second conference began August 1, 1745. The next morning we spoke of sanctification as follows;

Q. When does inward sanctification begin?

A. In the moment a person is justified. (Yet sin remains in him [or her]; yea the seed of all sin, till he [or she] is sanctified throughout.) From that time a believer gradually dies to sin, and grows in grace.

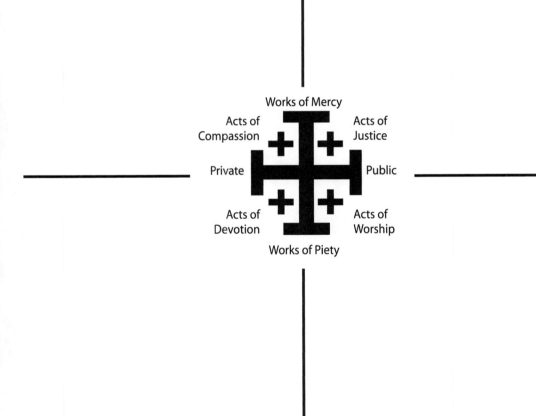

Works of Mercy

Acts of
Compassion

Acts of
Justice

Private

Public

Acts of
Devotion

Acts of
Worship

Works of Piety

To witness to Jesus Christ in the world and to follow his teachings
through acts of compassion, justice, worship, and devotion under the guidance of the Holy Spirit.

Psalm 23

Monday
1 John 3:16-24
John 10:1-5

Tuesday
Acts 4:1-12
John 10:6-10

Wednesday
Acts 4:13-22
John 10:11-18

Thursday
Acts 4:23-31
John 10:22-30

Friday
Ezekiel 34:1-10
1 Peter 2:1-10

Saturday
1 Peter 2:11-17
1 Peter 2:19-25

Sunday
John 10:11-18
Acts 5:12-32

Hymn: "Savior, Like a Shepherd Lead Us" (UMH 381)

PRAYER Concerns

A Word from John Wesley

Q. But are there any . . . [promises of deliverance from all sin] found in the New Testament?

A. There are. They are written in plain language: "The Son of God was revealed for this purpose, to destroy the works of the devil" (1 John 3:8c); the works of the devil without any limitation or restriction, but all sin is the work of the devil. Parallel to this is St. Paul's assertion: " . . . Christ loved the church and gave himself up for her, in order to make her holy by cleansing her with the washing of water by the word, so as to present the church to himself in splendor, without a spot or wrinkle or anything of the kind—yes, so that she may be holy and without blemish" (Ephesians 5:25b-27) . . .

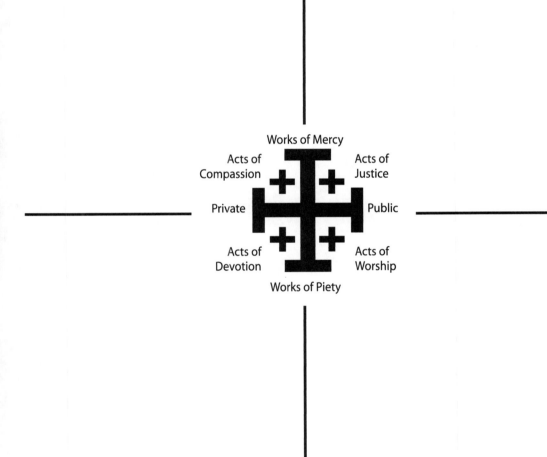

Works of Mercy

Acts of Compassion

Acts of Justice

Private

Public

Acts of Devotion

Acts of Worship

Works of Piety

To witness to Jesus Christ in the world and to follow his teachings
through acts of compassion, justice, worship, and devotion under the guidance of the Holy Spirit.

Psalm 22:25-31

Hymn: "Come, Let Us Use the Grace Divine" (UMH 606)

Monday
Acts 6
John 13:31-35

Tuesday
Acts 7:1–8:1a
John 14:1-14

Wednesday
Acts 8:1b-13
John 14:15-31

Thursday
Acts 8:14-25
John 15:1-8

Friday
Acts 8:26-40
1 John 4:1-6

Saturday
1 John 4:7-16a
1 John 4:16b-21

Sunday
Deuteronomy 4:32-40
1 John 5:1-6

PRAYER Concerns

A Word from John Wesley

Q. What is Christian perfection?

A. Christian perfection is the loving God with all our heart, mind, soul, and strength. This implies that no passions contrary to love remain in the soul. It means that all the thoughts, words, and actions, are governed by pure love.

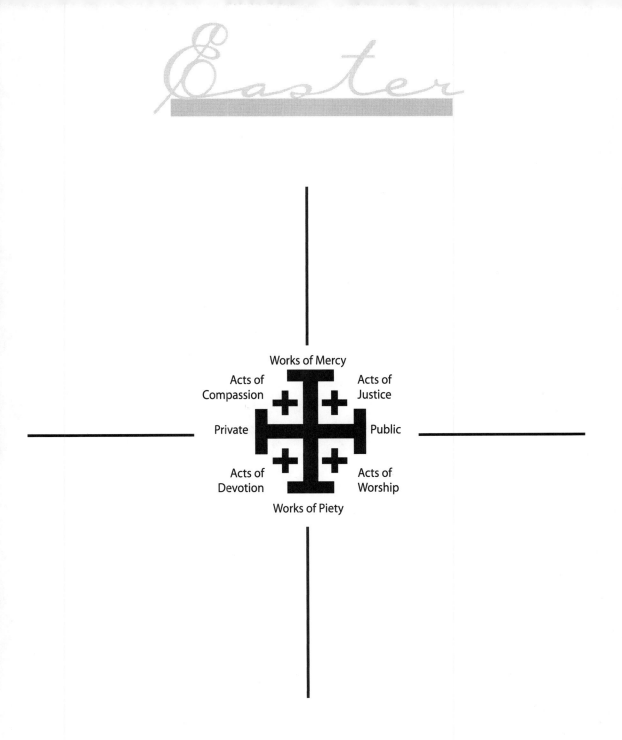

Works of Mercy

Acts of
Compassion

Acts of
Justice

Private

Public

Acts of
Devotion

Acts of
Worship

Works of Piety

To witness to Jesus Christ in the world and to follow his teachings
through acts of compassion, justice, worship, and devotion under the guidance of the Holy Spirit.

Psalm 98

Hymn: "Help Us Accept Each Other" (UMH 560)

Monday
Acts 9:1-9
John 15:9-17

Tuesday
Acts 9:10-31
John 15:18–16:4a

Wednesday
Acts 9:32-43
John 16:4b-11

Thursday
Acts 10:1-23a
John 16:12-15

Friday
Acts 10:23b-48
John 16:16-24

Saturday
Isaiah 45:11-13, 18-19
John 16:25-33

Sunday
John 15:9-17
Ezekiel 1:1-5a, 15-22; 1:26–2:2

PRAYER Concerns

A Word from John Wesley

None feel their need of Christ like [those who are perfected in love], none so entirely depend upon Him. For Christ does not give life to the soul separate from, but in and with, Himself. Hence his words are equally true of all people, in whatever state of grace they are: 'As the branch cannot bear fruit of itself, except it abide in the vine, no more can you, except you abide in Me. Without (or separate from) Me you can do nothing.

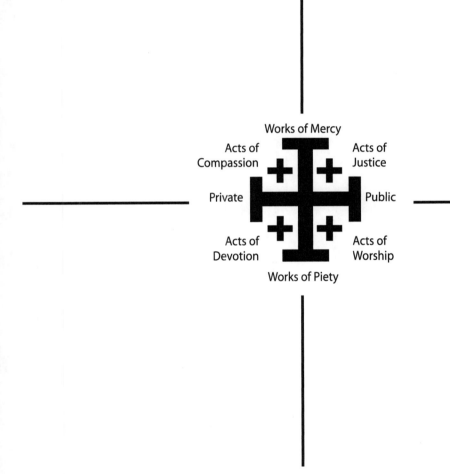

Works of Mercy

Acts of
Compassion

Acts of
Justice

Private

Public

Acts of
Devotion

Acts of
Worship

Works of Piety

To witness to Jesus Christ in the world and to follow his teachings
through acts of compassion, justice, worship, and devotion under the guidance of the Holy Spirit.

Psalm 47

Hymn: "Hail the Day That Sees Him Rise" (UMH 312)

Monday
1 Peter 3:8-17
1 Peter 3:18-22

Tuesday
1 Peter 4
1 Peter 5

Wednesday
Luke 24:44-53
Ephesians 1:15-19

Thursday (Ascension)
Acts 1:1-11
Ephesians 1:20-23

Friday
Acts 1:12-26
Psalm 1
John 17:1-19

Saturday
1 John 5:6-13
John 17:20-26

Sunday
John 17:6-19
Revelation 22:12-21

Prayer Concerns

A Word from John Wesley

In every state we need Christ in the following respects: 1) Whatever grace we receive, it is a free gift from Him. 2) We receive it as His purchase, merely in consideration of the price he paid. 3) We have this grace, not only from Christ, but in Him. For our perfection is not like that of a tree, which flourishes by the sap derived from its own root, but, as was said before, like that of a branch, which, united to the vine bears fruit. But, severed from it, is dried up and withered.

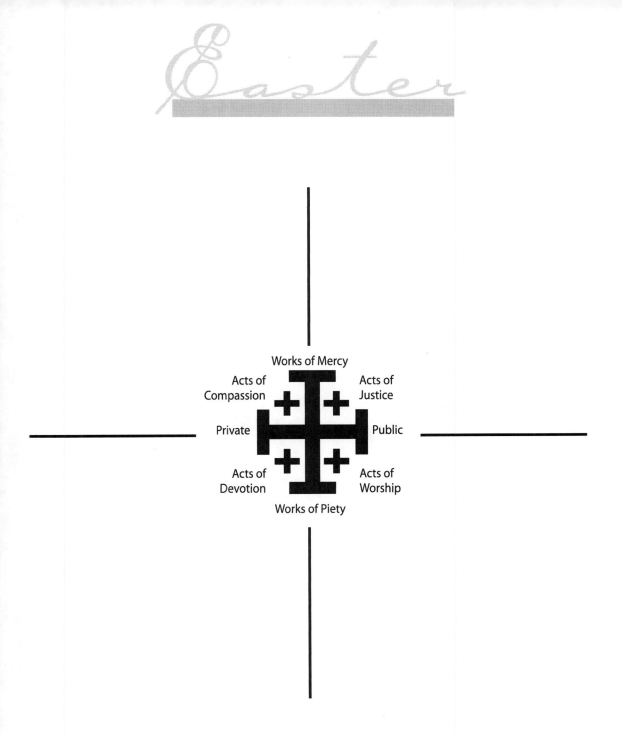

Works of Mercy

Acts of
Compassion

Acts of
Justice

Private

Public

Acts of
Devotion

Acts of
Worship

Works of Piety

To witness to Jesus Christ in the world and to follow his teachings
through acts of compassion, justice, worship, and devotion under the guidance of the Holy Spirit.

Psalm 104:24-35

Hymn: "See How Great a Flame Aspires" (UMH 541)

Monday
Genesis 11:1-9
Acts 2:1-11

Tuesday
Joel 2:28-32
Acts 2:12-21

Wednesday
Romans 8:1-11
John 7:37-39

Thursday
Romans 8:18-27
John 14:15-17, 25-27

Friday
1 Corinthians 12:1-13
John 15:26-27; 16:4b-15

Saturday
Galatians 5:16-26
John 20:19-23

Sunday (Pentecost)
Acts 2:1-21
Genesis 1:1-5

PRAYER Concerns

A Word from John Wesley

All our blessings, temporal, spiritual, and eternal, depend on His intercession for us, which is one branch of His priestly office, where therefore we always have equal need. 5) The best of people still need Christ, in His priestly office, to atone for their omissions, their shortcomings (as some not improperly speak), their mistakes in judgment and practice, and their defects of various kinds, for these are all deviations from the perfect law and consequently need an atonement.

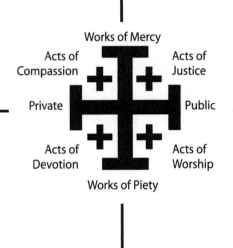

Works of Mercy

Acts of Compassion

Acts of Justice

Private

Public

Acts of Devotion

Acts of Worship

Works of Piety

To witness to Jesus Christ in the world and to follow his teachings
through acts of compassion, justice, worship, and devotion under the guidance of the Holy Spirit.

Psalm 29

Monday
Genesis 1:6-8
Romans 8:12-17

Tuesday
Genesis 1:9-13
Isaiah 6:1-8

Wednesday
Genesis 1:14-19
John 3:1-17

Thursday
Genesis 1:20-23
Matthew 28:16-20

Friday
Genesis 1:24-31
John 16:12-15

Saturday
Genesis 2:1-4a
Romans 5:1-5

Sunday
John 3:1-17
2 Corinthians 13:11-13

Hymn: "Maker, in Whom We Live" (UMH 88)

PRAYER Concerns

A Word from John Wesley

Now, mistakes and whatever infirmities necessarily flow from the corruptible state of the body are no way contrary to love; nor therefore, in the Scripture sense, sin.

To explain myself a little farther—(1) Not only sin, properly so called (that is, a voluntary transgression of a known law), but sin, improperly so called (that is, an involuntary transgression of a divine law, known or unknown) needs the atoning blood.

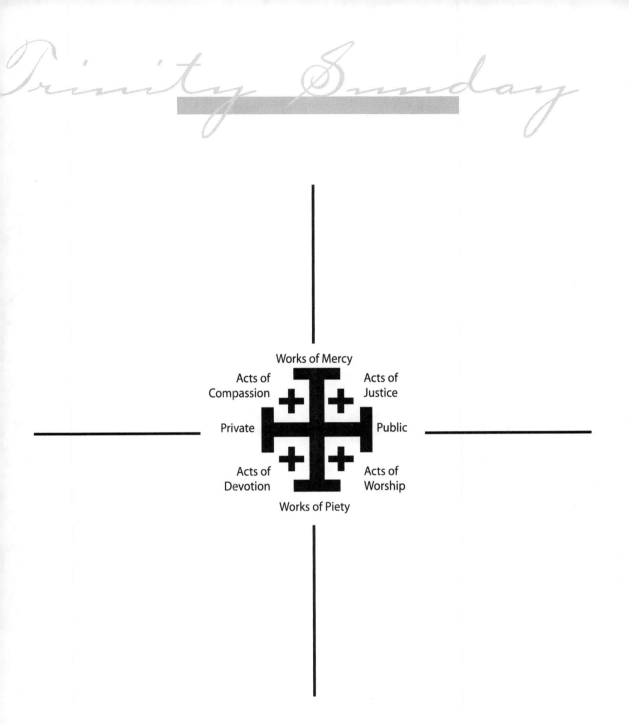

To witness to Jesus Christ in the world and to follow his teachings
through acts of compassion, justice, worship, and devotion under the guidance of the Holy Spirit.

Psalm 103:1-13, 22

Monday
   Hosea 2:14-20
   Mark 1:29-39

Tuesday
   2 Corinthians 1:1-11
   Mark 1:40-45

Wednesday
   2 Corinthians 1:12-22
   Mark 2:1-12

Thursday
   2 Corinthians 1:23–2:13
   Mark 2:18-20

Friday
   2 Corinthians 2:14–3:6
   Mark 2:13-17

Saturday
   2 Corinthians 3:7-18
   1 Samuel 1:1-18

Sunday
   Mark 2:21-22
   1 Samuel 1:19-28

Hymn: "Heal Me, Hands of Jesus" (UMH 262)

PRAYER Concerns

A Word from John Wesley

Q. But what does the perfect one do more than others?

A. Perhaps nothing, so may the providence of God have hedged him in by outward circumstances. Perhaps not so much, though he desires and longs to spend and be spent for God-at least, not externally. He neither speaks so many words, nor does so many works, as neither did our Lord Himself speak so many words, or do so many, no nor so great works, as some of His apostles (John 14:12).

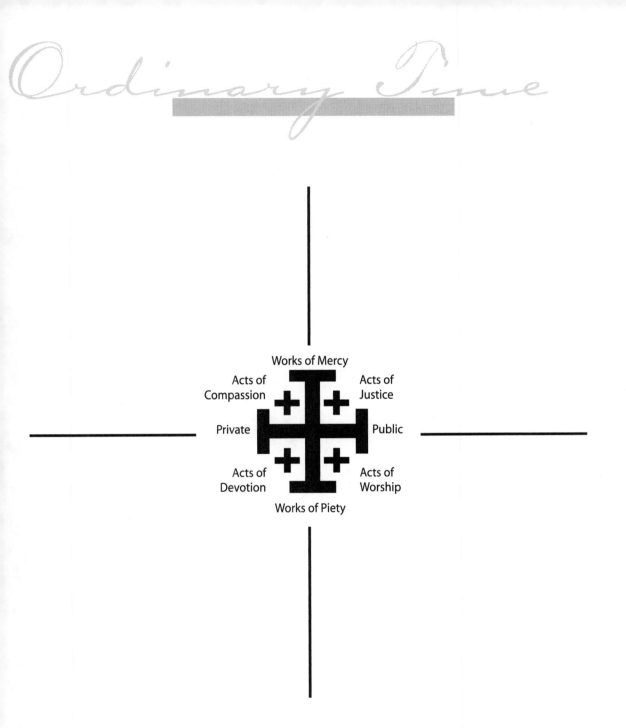

Works of Mercy

Acts of
Compassion

Acts of
Justice

Private

Public

Acts of
Devotion

Acts of
Worship

Works of Piety

To witness to Jesus Christ in the world and to follow his teachings
through acts of compassion, justice, worship, and devotion under the guidance of the Holy Spirit.

Psalm 139:1-6, 13-18

Hymn: "Lord of the Dance" (UMH 261)

Monday
1 Samuel 2:1-10
2 Corinthians 4:1-7

Tuesday
1 Samuel 2:11-36
2 Corinthians 4:8-12

Wednesday
1 Samuel 3:1-20
Mark 2:23-28

Thursday
1 Samuel 3:21–4:1a
Mark 3:1-6

Friday
1 Samuel 4:1b-22
2 Corinthians 4:5-12

Saturday
1 Samuel 5
1 Samuel 6:1–7:2

Sunday
Mark 2:23–3:6
1 Samuel 7:3-17

Prayer Concerns

A Word from John Wesley

But he does not come up to my idea of a perfect Christian." And perhaps no one ever did, or ever will. For your idea may go beyond, or at least beside, the scriptural account. It may include more than the Bible includes therein; or, however, something which that does not include. Scripture perfection is pure love, filling the heart, and governing all the words and actions. If your idea includes anything more or anything else, it is not scriptural; and then, no wonder that a scripturally perfect Christian does not come up to it.

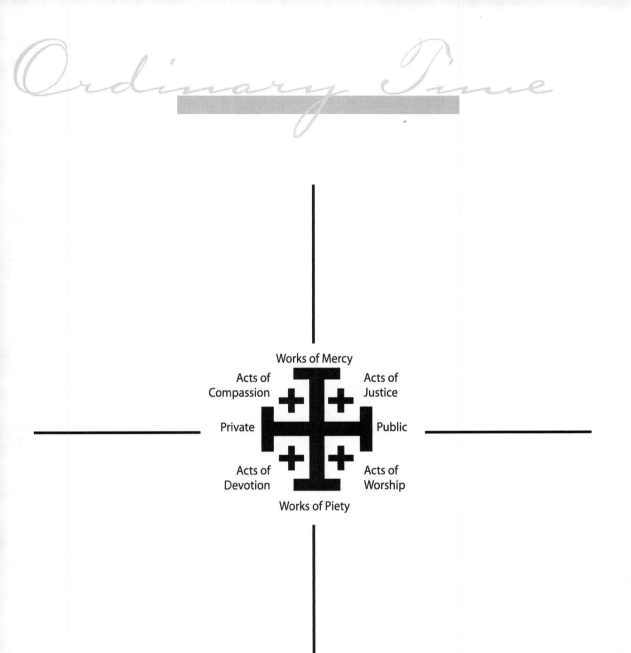

Works of Mercy

Acts of Compassion

Acts of Justice

Private

Public

Acts of Devotion

Acts of Worship

Works of Piety

To witness to Jesus Christ in the world and to follow his teachings
through acts of compassion, justice, worship, and devotion under the guidance of the Holy Spirit.

Psalm 138

Hymn: "Christ Is the World's Light" (UMH 188)

Monday
1 Samuel 8
2 Corinthians 4:13-18

Tuesday
1 Samuel 9:1–10:16
2 Corinthians 5:1-5

Wednesday
1 Samuel 10:17-27a
Mark 3:7-19

Thursday
1 Samuel 10:27b–11:15
Mark 3:20-30

Friday
1 Samuel 12
Mark 3:31-35

Saturday
1 Samuel 13:1-22
1 Samuel 13:23–14:23

Sunday
Mark 3:20-35
1 Samuel 14:24-52

PRAYER Concerns

A Word from John Wesley

Q. When may a person judge himself to have attained [perfection in love].

A. When, after having been fully convinced of inbred sin, by a far deeper and clearer conviction than that he experienced before justification, and after having experienced a gradual mortification of it, he experiences a total death to sin, and an entire renewal in the love and image of God, as to rejoice evermore, to pray without ceasing, and in everything to give thanks. Not that "to feel all love and no sin" is a sufficient proof . . . None therefore out to believe that the work is done, till there is added the testimony of the Spirit witnessing his entire sanctification as clearly as his justification.

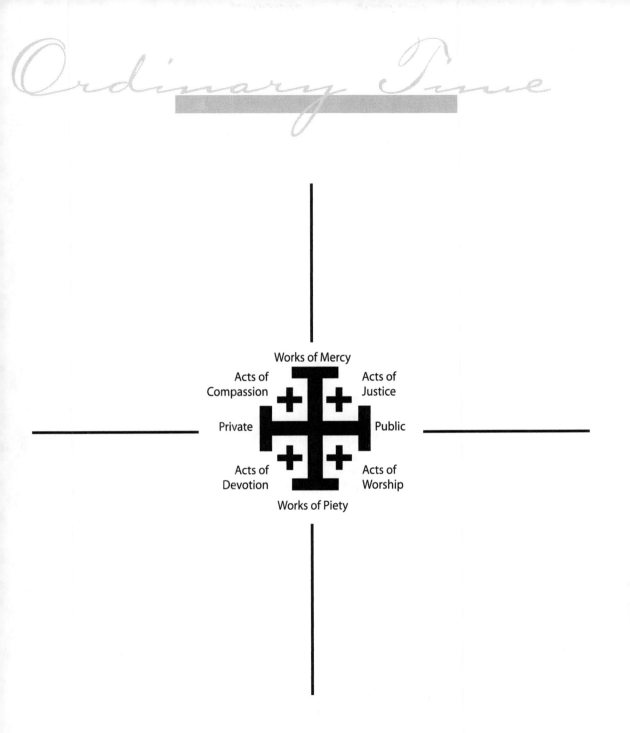

Works of Mercy

Acts of
Compassion

Acts of
Justice

Private

Public

Acts of
Devotion

Acts of
Worship

Works of Piety

To witness to Jesus Christ in the world and to follow his teachings
through acts of compassion, justice, worship, and devotion under the guidance of the Holy Spirit.

Psalm 20

Hymn: "Rejoice, the Lord Is King" (UMH 715)

Monday
2 Corinthians 5:6-15
Mark 4:1-20

Tuesday
2 Corinthians 5:16-21
Mark 4:21-25

Wednesday
1 Samuel 15:1-31
Mark 4:26-29

Thursday
1 Samuel 15:34–16:13

Friday
1 Samuel 16:14-23
2 Corinthians 5:6-15

Saturday
2 Corinthians 5:16-21
Mark 4:26-29

Sunday
Mark 4:30-34
1 Samuel 17:1-11

PRAYER Concerns

A Word from John Wesley

Q. How are we to wait for this change?

A. Not in careless indifference, or indolent inactivity; but in vigorous, universal obedience, in a zealous keeping of all the commandments, in watchfulness and painfulness, in denying ourselves, and taking up our cross daily; as well as in earnest prayer and fasting, and a close attendance on all the ordinances of God. And if any man dream of attaining it any other way (yea, or of keeping it when it is attained, when he has received it even in the largest measure), he deceives his own soul. It is true, we receive it by simple faith, but God does not, will not, give that faith unless we seek it with all diligence, in the way which He has ordained.

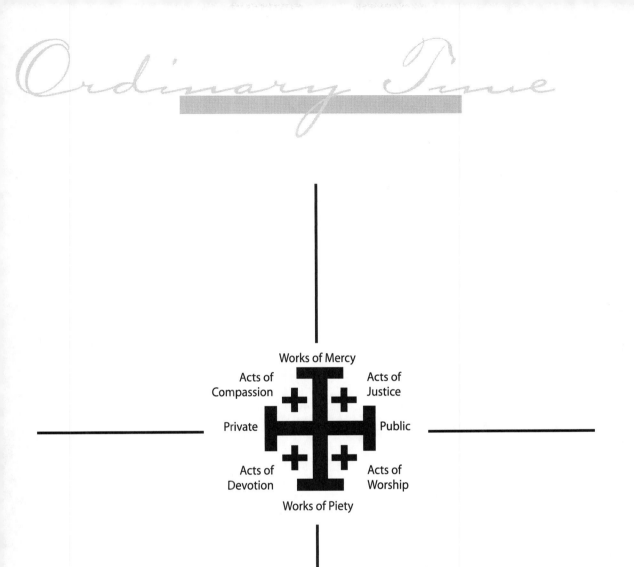

To witness to Jesus Christ in the world and to follow his teachings
through acts of compassion, justice, worship, and devotion under the guidance of the Holy Spirit.

Psalm 9:9-20

Hymn: "Stand By Me" (UMH 512)

Monday
    1 Samuel 17:12-37
    2 Corinthians 6:1-2

Tuesday
    1 Samuel 17:38-58
    2 Corinthians 6:3-13

Wednesday
    1 Samuel 18:1-5
    Mark 4:35-41

Thursday
    1 Samuel 18:6-30
    2 Corinthians 6:14–7:1

Friday
    1 Samuel 19
    2 Corinthians 7:2-16

Saturday
    1 Samuel 20
    1 Samuel 21

Sunday
    Mark 4:35-41
    1 Samuel 22:1–23:14

Prayer Concerns

A Word from John Wesley

Q. But may we not continue in peace and joy till we are perfected in love?

A. Certainly we may; for the kingdom of God is not divided against itself; therefore let not believers be discouraged from "rejoicing in the Lord always." And yet we may be sensibly pained at the sinful nature that still remains in us. It is good for us to have a piercing sense of this, and a vehement desire to be delivered from it. But this should only incite us the more zealously to fly every moment to our strong Helper; the more earnestly to "press forward to the mark, the prize of our high calling in Christ Jesus." And when the sense of our sin most abounds, the sense of His love should much more abound.

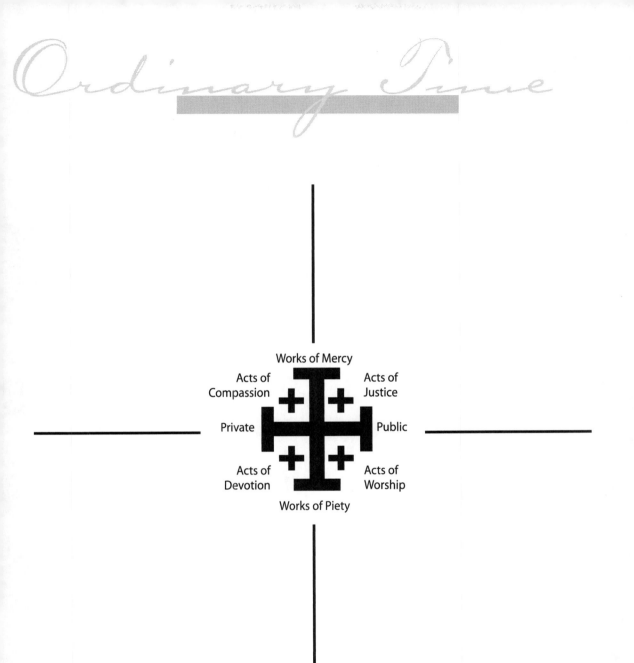

Works of Mercy

Acts of
Compassion

Acts of
Justice

Private

Public

Acts of
Devotion

Acts of
Worship

Works of Piety

To witness to Jesus Christ in the world and to follow his teachings
through acts of compassion, justice, worship, and devotion under the guidance of the Holy Spirit.

Psalm 130

Monday
1 Samuel 23:15–24:22
Mark 5:1-20

Tuesday
1 Samuel 25
Mark 5:21-43

Wednesday
1 Samuel 26
2 Corinthians 8

Thursday
1 Samuel 27
1 Samuel 28

Friday
1 Samuel 29
1 Samuel 30

Saturday
1 Samuel 31
2 Samuel 1

Sunday
Mark 5:21-43
2 Corinthians 9

Hymn: "Let Us Plead for Faith Alone" (UMH 385)

Prayer Concerns

A Word from John Wesley

Q. How, then, are we "not without law to God, but under the law to Christ" (1 Corinthians. 9:21)?

A. We are without that law; but it does not follow that we are without any law, for God has established another law in its place, even the law of faith. And we are all under this law to God and to Christ. Both our Creator and our Redeemer require us to observe it.

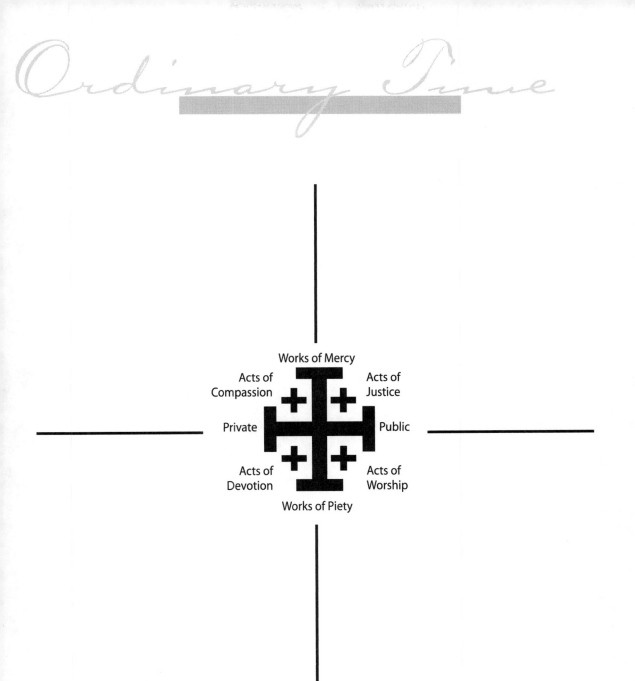

Works of Mercy

Acts of
Compassion

Acts of
Justice

Private

Public

Acts of
Devotion

Acts of
Worship

Works of Piety

To witness to Jesus Christ in the world and to follow his teachings
through acts of compassion, justice, worship, and devotion under the guidance of the Holy Spirit.

Psalm 48

Hymn: "Ye Servants of God" (UMH 181)

Monday
1 Chronicles 10
2 Corinthians 10

Tuesday
2 Samuel 2:1-11
2 Corinthians 11

Wednesday
2 Samuel 2:12-32
2 Corinthians 12:1-13

Thursday
2 Samuel 3
2 Corinthians 12:14–13:13

Friday
2 Samuel 4
Mark 6:1-6

Saturday
2 Samuel 5:1-10
Mark 6:7-13

Sunday
2 Corinthians 12:2-10
2 Samuel 5:11-16

PRAYER Concerns

A Word from John Wesley

Q. Is love the fulfilling of this law?

A. Unquestionably it is. The whole law under which we now are is fulfilled by love (Romans 13:8, 10). Faith working or animated by love is all that God now requires of man. He has substituted (not sincerity, but) love, in the room of angelic perfection.

Q. How is "love the end of the commandment" (1 Timothy. 1:5)?

A. It is the end of every commandment of God. It is the point aimed at by the whole and every part of the Christian institution. The foundation is faith, purifying the heart; the end, love, preserving a good conscience.

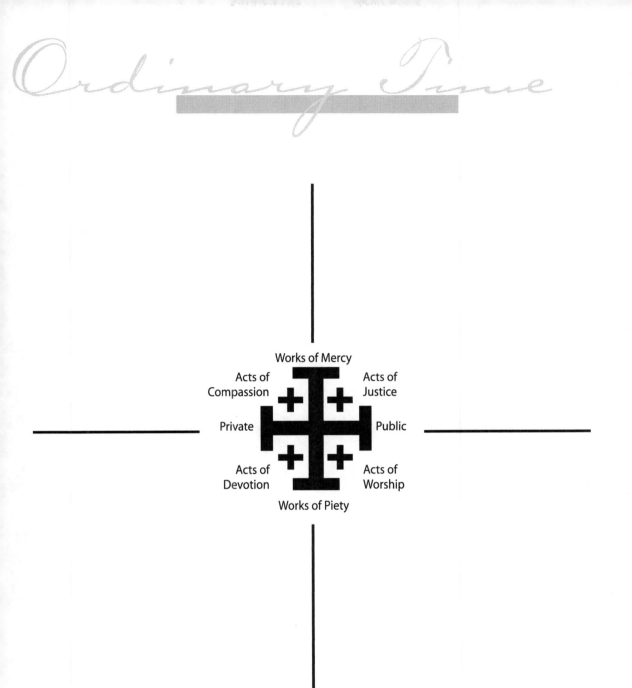

Works of Mercy

Acts of
Compassion

Acts of
Justice

Private

Public

Acts of
Devotion

Acts of
Worship

Works of Piety

To witness to Jesus Christ in the world and to follow his teachings
through acts of compassion, justice, worship, and devotion under the guidance of the Holy Spirit.

Psalm 24

Hymn: "Faith of Our Fathers" (UMH 710)

Monday
2 Samuel 5:17-25
Mark 6:14-16

Tuesday
1 Chronicles 11:1-9
Mark 6:17-29

Wednesday
2 Samuel 6:1-5
Ephesians 1:1-10

Thursday
2 Samuel 6:6-15
Ephesians 1:11-14

Friday
2 Samuel 6:16-23
Ephesians 1:15-19

Saturday
1 Chronicles 13
Ephesians 1:20-23

Sunday
Mark 6:14-29
1 Chronicles 15

PRAYER Concerns

A Word from John Wesley

Q. What love is this?

A. The loving the Lord our God with all our heart, mind, soul, and strength; and the loving our neighbor, every one, as ourselves, as our own souls.

Q. What are the fruits or properties of this love?

A. St. Paul informs us at large: "Love is patient." It suffers all the weaknesses of the children of God, all the wickedness of the children of the world; and that not for a little time only, but as long as God pleases. In all, it sees the hand of God, and willingly submits to it . . .

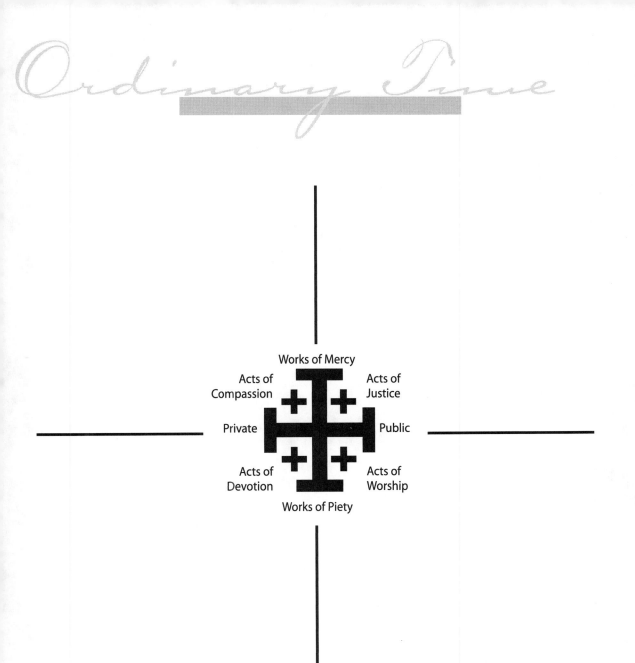

Works of Mercy

Acts of
Compassion

Acts of
Justice

Private

Public

Acts of
Devotion

Acts of
Worship

Works of Piety

To witness to Jesus Christ in the world and to follow his teachings
through acts of compassion, justice, worship, and devotion under the guidance of the Holy Spirit.

Psalm 89:20-37

Hymn: "Fill My Cup, Lord" (UMH 641)

Monday
Ephesians 2:1-7
Mark 6:30-34

Tuesday
Ephesians 2:8-10
Mark 6:35-46

Wednesday
Ephesians 2:11-22
Mark 6:47-52

Thursday
2 Samuel 7:1-14a
Mark 6:53-56

Friday
2 Samuel 7:12-17
2 Samuel 7:18-29

Saturday
1 Chronicles 16
1 Chronicles 17

Sunday
Mark 6:30-34, 53-56
John 4:43-45

PRAYER Concerns

A Word from John Wesley

Q. Do we not then need Christ, even on this account?

A. The holiest of men still need Christ as their Prophet, as "the light of the world." For He does not give them light but from moment to moment; the instant He withdraws, all is darkness. They still need Christ as their King; for God does not give them a stock of holiness. But unless they receive a supply every moment, nothing but unholiness would remain. They still need Christ as their Priest, to make atonement for their holy things. Even perfect holiness is acceptable to God only through Jesus Christ.

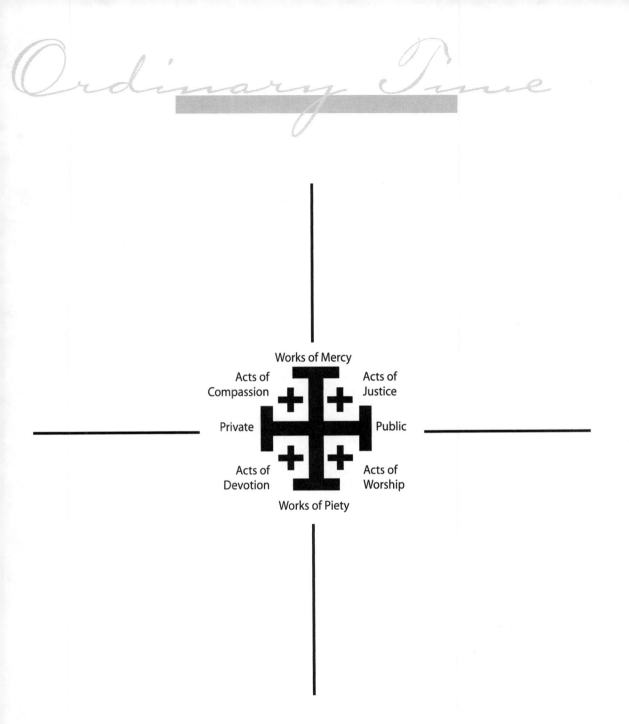

Works of Mercy

Acts of
Compassion

Acts of
Justice

Private

Public

Acts of
Devotion

Acts of
Worship

Works of Piety

To witness to Jesus Christ in the world and to follow his teachings
through acts of compassion, justice, worship, and devotion under the guidance of the Holy Spirit.

Psalm 14

Monday
Ephesians 3:1-13
John 4:46-54

Tuesday
Ephesians 3:14-17
John 5:1-18

Wednesday
Ephesians 3:18-21
John 5:19-24

Thursday
2 Samuel 9
John 5:25-47

Friday
2 Samuel 10
John 6:1-15

Saturday
2 Samuel 11:1-15
John 6:16-21

Sunday
Ephesians 3:14-21
2 Samuel 11:16-25

Hymn: "Spirit Song" (UMH 347)

PRAYER Concerns

A Word from John Wesley

Q. May not, then, the very best of people adopt the dying martyr's confession: "I am in myself nothing but sin, darkness, hell; but Thou art my light, my holiness, my heaven?"

A. Not exactly. But the best of people may say, "Thou art my light, my holiness, my heaven. Through my union with Thee, I am full of light, of holiness, and happiness. But if I were left to myself, I should be nothing but sin, darkness, hell."

But to proceed: the best of people need Christ as their Priest, their Atonement, their Advocate with the Father; not only as the continuance of their every blessing depends on His death and intercession, but on account of their coming short of the law of love.

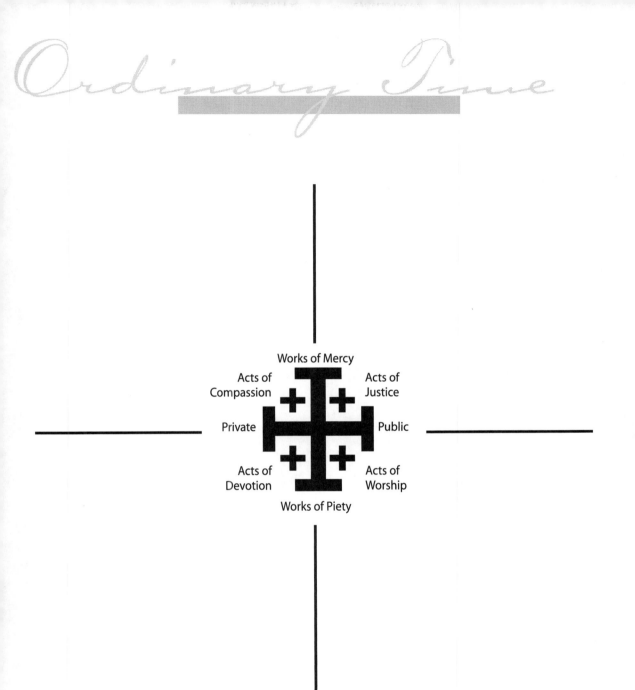

Works of Mercy

Acts of Compassion

Acts of Justice

Private

Public

Acts of Devotion

Acts of Worship

Works of Piety

To witness to Jesus Christ in the world and to follow his teachings
through acts of compassion, justice, worship, and devotion under the guidance of the Holy Spirit.

Psalm 51:1-12

Hymn: "Come, Sinners, to the Gospel Feast" (UMH 339)

Monday
2 Samuel 11:26–12:13a
John 6:22-27

Tuesday
2 Samuel 12:13b-25
John 6:28-35

Wednesday
2 Samuel 13:1-22
Ephesians 4:7-16

Thursday
2 Samuel 13:23-39
Ephesians 4:1-6

Friday
2 Samuel 14:1-24
2 Samuel 14:25-33

Saturday
2 Samuel 15:1-23
2 Samuel 15:24-37

Sunday
John 6:24-35
2 Samuel 16

PRAYER Concerns

A Word from John Wesley

Q. Does, then, Christian perfection imply any more than sincerity?

A. Not if you mean by that word, love filling the heart, expelling pride, anger, desire, self-will, rejoicing evermore, praying without ceasing, and in everything giving thanks. But I doubt few use sincerity in this sense. Therefore, I think the old word is best.

A person may be sincere who has all their natural tempers-pride, anger, lust, self-will. But he or she is not perfect till his or her heart is cleansed from these, and all its other corruptions.

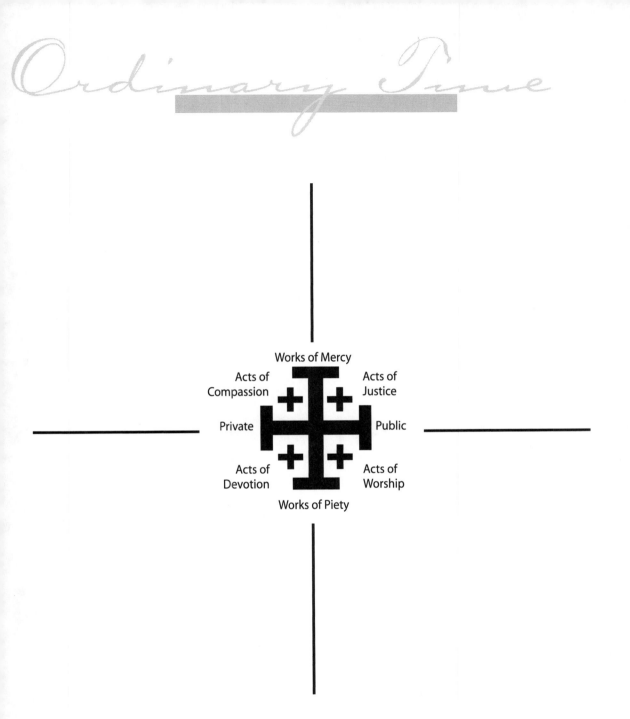

Works of Mercy

Acts of Compassion

Acts of Justice

Private

Public

Acts of Devotion

Acts of Worship

Works of Piety

To witness to Jesus Christ in the world and to follow his teachings
through acts of compassion, justice, worship, and devotion under the guidance of the Holy Spirit.

Psalm 130

Hymn: "Eat This Bread" (UMH 628)

Monday
2 Samuel 17
John 6:35-40

Tuesday
2 Samuel 18:1-18
John 6:41-47

Wednesday
2 Samuel 18:19-33
John 6:48-51

Thursday
2 Samuel 19
Ephesians 4:17-24

Friday
2 Samuel 20
Ephesians 4:25–5:2

Saturday
2 Samuel 22:1-25
2 Samuel 22:26-51

Sunday
John 6:35, 41-51
2 Samuel 23:1-7

PRAYER Concerns

A Word from John Wesley

Q. But how do you know that you are sanctified, saved from your inbred corruption?

A. I can know it no otherwise than I know that I am justified. "Hereby know we that we are of God," in either sense "by the Spirit that He hath given us."

We know it by the witness and by the fruit of the Spirit. And, first, by the witness. As, when we were justified, the Spirit bore witness with our spirit that our sins were forgiven; so, when we were sanctified, He bore witness that they were taken away. Indeed, the witness of sanctification is not always clear at first (as neither is that of justification); neither is it afterward always the same, but, like that of justification, sometimes stronger, and sometimes fainter. Yea, and sometimes it is withdrawn. Yet, in general, the latter testimony of the Spirit is both as clear and as steady as the former.

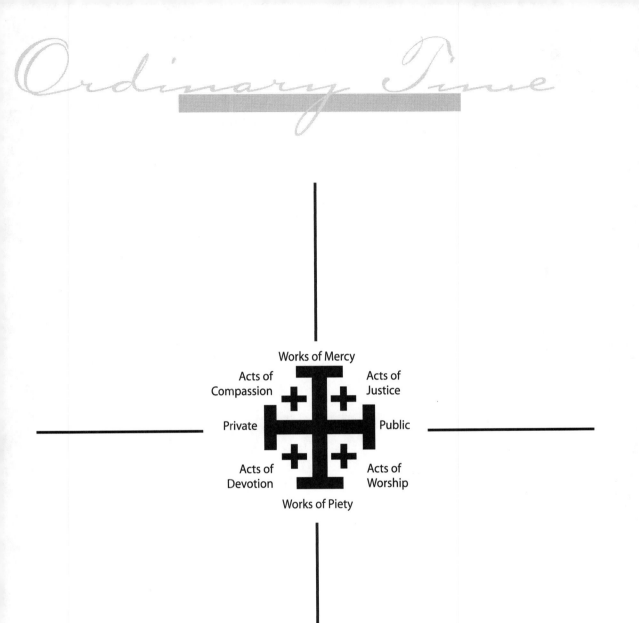

To witness to Jesus Christ in the world and to follow his teachings
through acts of compassion, justice, worship, and devotion under the guidance of the Holy Spirit.

Psalm 111

Hymn: "Here, O My Lord, I See Thee" (UMH 623)

Monday
  1 Kings 1:1-31
  John 6:51-58

Tuesday
  1 Kings 1:32-53
  Ephesians 5:3-14

Wednesday
  1 Kings 2:1-12
  Ephesians 5:15-20

Thursday
  1 Chronicles 29:10-19
  Ephesians 5:21-33

Friday
  1 Chronicles 29:20-30
  Ephesians 6:1-9

Saturday
  1 Kings 2:13-46
  1 Kings 3:3-15

Sunday
  John 6:51-68
  1 Kings 3:16-28

PRAYER Concerns

A Word from John Wesley

Q. But is not this the case of all that are justified? Do they not gradually die to sin and grow in grace, till, at or perhaps a little before death, God perfects them in love?

A. I believe this is the case of most, but not all. God usually gives a considerable time for people to receive light, to grow in grace, to do and suffer His will, before they are either justified or sanctified; but He does not invariably adhere to this; sometimes He "cuts short His work." He does the work of many years in a few weeks; perhaps in a week, a day, an hour. He justifies or sanctifies both those who have done or suffered nothing, and who have not had time for a gradual growth either in light or grace.

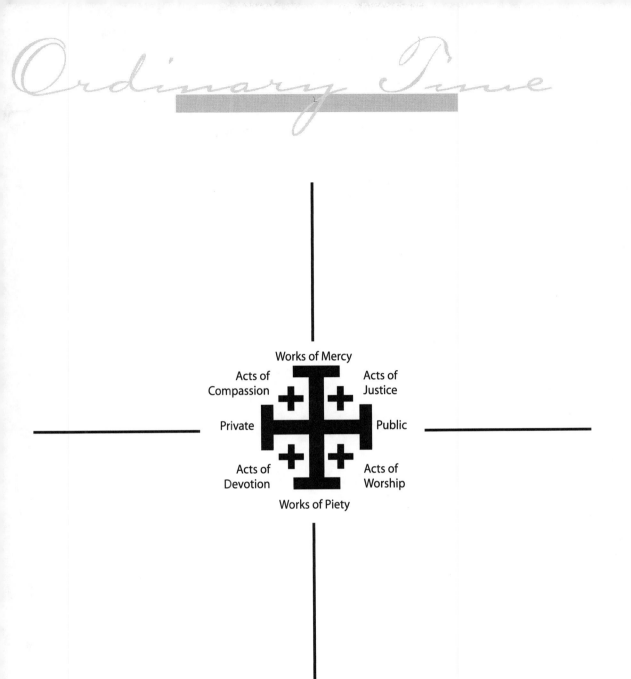

Works of Mercy

Acts of
Compassion

Acts of
Justice

Private

Public

Acts of
Devotion

Acts of
Worship

Works of Piety

To witness to Jesus Christ in the world and to follow his teachings
through acts of compassion, justice, worship, and devotion under the guidance of the Holy Spirit.

Psalm 84

Hymn: "Spirit of Faith, Come Down" (UMH 332)

Monday
1 Kings 5
John 6:56-71

Tuesday
1 Kings 6:1-14
Ephesians 6:10-24

Wednesday
1 Kings 7:51–8:21
1 Kings 8:22-43

Thursday
1 Kings 8:54-66
2 Chronicles 2

Friday
1 Kings 9:1-9
1 Kings 10:1-13

Saturday
1 Kings 11:1-13
1 Kings 11:14-42

Sunday
Ephesians 6:10-20
Song of Solomon 1:1–2:2

PRAYER Concerns

A Word from John Wesley

Q. But how can those who are sealed in this way 'grieve the Holy Spirit of God?

A. St. Paul tells you very particularly,
1. By conversation that is not beneficial, edifying, or likely to minister grace to the hearers.
2. By relapsing into bitterness or lack of kindness.
3. By wrath, lasting displeasure, or lack of tender-heartedness.
4. By anger, however soon it is over; lack of instantly forgiving one another.
5. By bluster or bawling, loud, harsh, rough speaking,

By evil-speaking, whispering, gossiping; needlessly mentioning the fault of an absent person, though in ever so soft a manner.

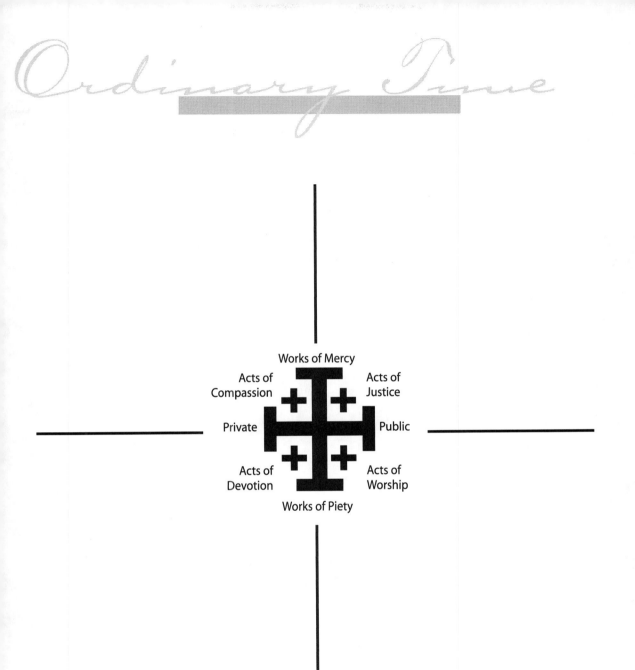

Works of Mercy

Acts of
Compassion

Acts of
Justice

Private

Public

Acts of
Devotion

Acts of
Worship

Works of Piety

To witness to Jesus Christ in the world and to follow his teachings
through acts of compassion, justice, worship, and devotion under the guidance of the Holy Spirit.

Psalm 45:1-2, 6-9

Hymn: "O For a Thousand Tongues to Sing" (UMH 57)

Monday
Song of Solomon 2:3-17
Mark 7:1-8

Tuesday
Song of Solomon 3
Mark 7:9-16

Wednesday
Song of Solomon 4:1–5:1
Mark 7:17-23

Thursday
Song of Solomon 5:2–6:3
James 1:1-8

Friday
Song of Solomon 6:4-12
James 1:9-18

Saturday
Song of Solomon 6:13–8:4
James 1:19-27

Sunday
Mark 7:1-8, 14-15, 21-23
Song of Solomon 8:5-14

PRAYER Concerns

A Word from John Wesley

Q. Can those who are perfect grow in grace?

A. Certainly they can, not only in this life, but the life to come.

Q. Can they fall from it?

A. I am certain they can. The reason and experience put this beyond dispute. Previously we thought that one who was saved from sin could not fall. But now we know this is not true. We are surrounded with examples of those who recently experienced all that I mean by perfection. They had both the fruit and the witness of the Spirit. But now they have lost both. No one may ever expect to stand by virtue of anything implied in the nature of Christian perfection. There is no height or strength of holiness from which it is impossible to fall. If there is any that cannot fall, this depends completely upon the promise of God.

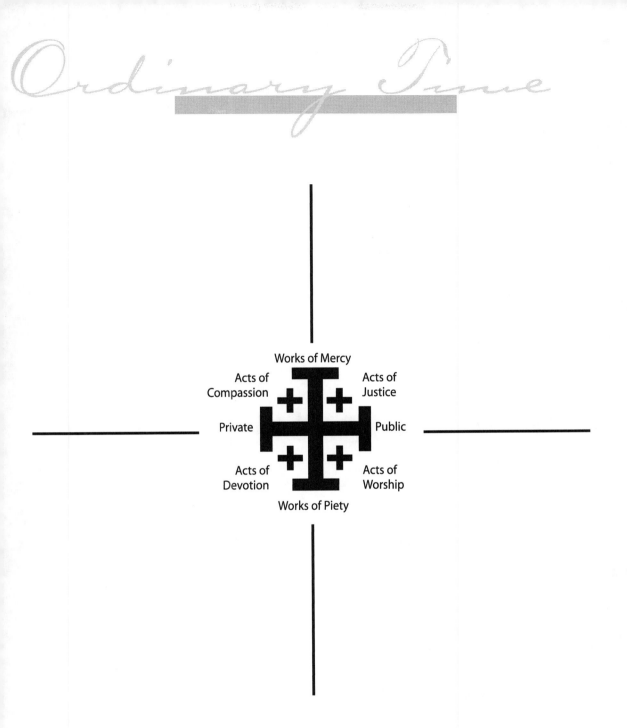

Works of Mercy

Acts of
Compassion

Acts of
Justice

Private

Public

Acts of
Devotion

Acts of
Worship

Works of Piety

To witness to Jesus Christ in the world and to follow his teachings
through acts of compassion, justice, worship, and devotion under the guidance of the Holy Spirit.

Psalm 125

Hymn: "Rise, Shine, You People" (UMH 187)

Monday
Proverbs 8:1, 22-36
Mark 7:24-30

Tuesday
Proverbs 9:1-10
Mark 7:1-37

Wednesday
Proverbs 14:29–15:5; 16:16-19
James 2:1-7

Thursday
Proverbs 22:1-23
James 2:8-9

Friday
Proverbs 23:10-11, 19-21, 29-35
James 2:10-13

Saturday
Proverbs 25:21-22; 27:1-6
James 2:14-17

Sunday
James 2:18-27
James 3:1-5a

PRAYER
Concerns

A Word from John Wesley

Q. Can those who fall from this state recover it?

A. Why not? We have many instances of this also. Indeed, it is very common for persons to lose it more than once before they are established in it.

It is therefore to protect the ones who are saved from sin and from every occasion of stumbling, that I give the following words of advice.

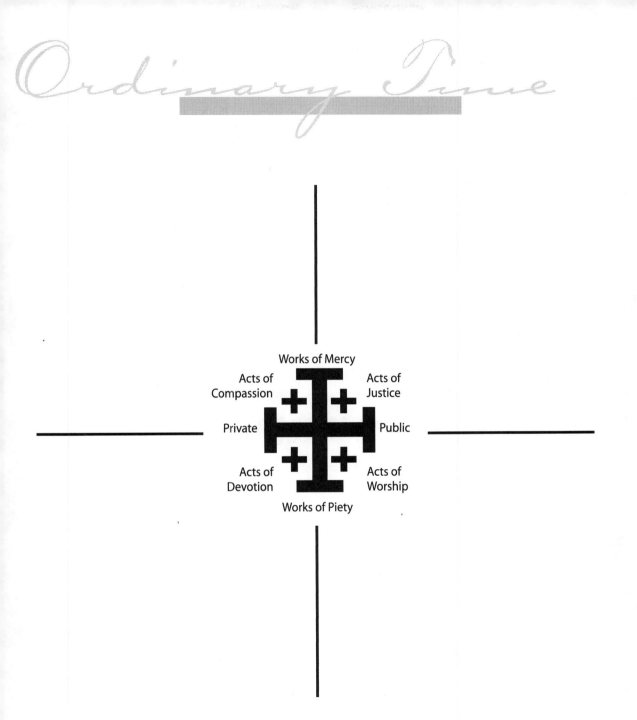

Works of Mercy

Acts of
Compassion

Acts of
Justice

Private

Public

Acts of
Devotion

Acts of
Worship

Works of Piety

To witness to Jesus Christ in the world and to follow his teachings
through acts of compassion, justice, worship, and devotion under the guidance of the Holy Spirit.

Psalm 19

Monday
James 3:5b-12
Mark 8:27-38

Tuesday
Proverbs 1:1-10
Mark 8:1-10

Wednesday
Proverbs 1:20-33
Mark 8:11-13

Thursday
Proverbs 2
Mark 8:14-21

Friday
Proverbs 3:9-20, 27-32
Mark 8:22-26

Saturday
Proverbs 4:1-13
Mark 8:27-33

Sunday
Mark 8:34–9:1
Proverbs 6:6-19

Hymn: "Come, O Thou Traveler Unknown"
(UMH 386 and 387)

PRAYER Concerns

A Word from John Wesley

Q. What is the first advice that you would give them?

A. Beware of and pray constantly against pride. If God has cast it out, see that it does not return. It is every bit as dangerous as desire. When you think there is no danger, you may slide back into it without notice.

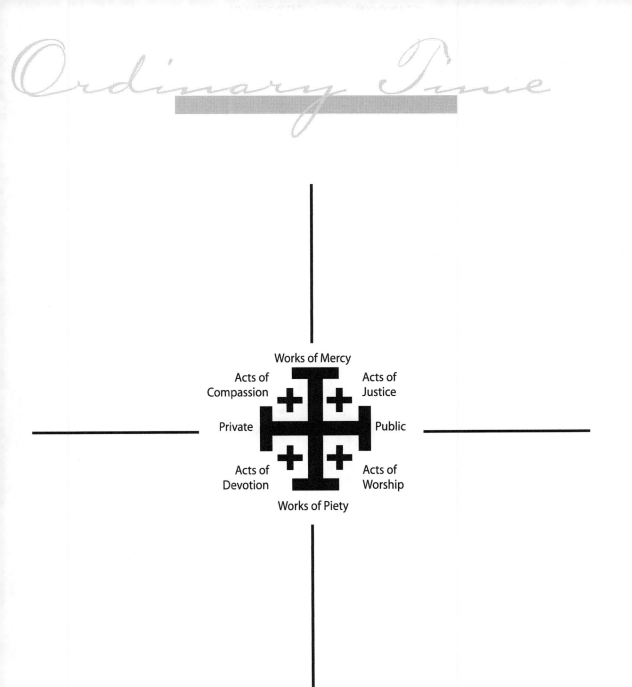

To witness to Jesus Christ in the world and to follow his teachings
through acts of compassion, justice, worship, and devotion under the guidance of the Holy Spirit.

Psalm 1

Hymn: "Jesus, United by Thy Grace" (UMH 561)

Monday
James 3:13-18
Mark 9:30-37

Tuesday
James 4:1-10
Mark 9:2-8

Wednesday
James 4:11-12
Mark 9:9-13

Thursday
Proverbs 31:1-9
Mark 9:14-29

Friday
Proverbs 31:10-31
Mark 9:30-32

Saturday
Proverbs 28:1-16
Mark 3:33-37

Sunday
James 4:13-17
James 5:1-6

PRAYER Concerns

A Word from John Wesley

You may say, "Indeed, but I credit all I have to God." You may do so and be proud nevertheless. For it is pride not only to credit anything we have to ourselves, but to think we have what we really do not have. For example, Mr. L credited all the light he had to God, and so far he was humble. But then he thought he had more light than any man living. This was palpable pride. So you credit all the knowledge you have to God and, in this respect, you are humble. But if you think you have more than you really have, or if you think you are so knowledgeable of God as to no longer need man's teaching, then pride is at the door.

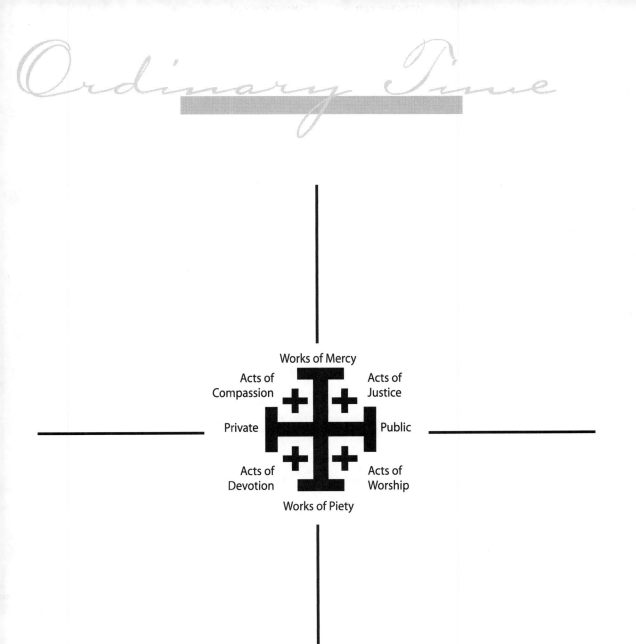

Works of Mercy

Acts of
Compassion

Acts of
Justice

Private

Public

Acts of
Devotion

Acts of
Worship

Works of Piety

To witness to Jesus Christ in the world and to follow his teachings
through acts of compassion, justice, worship, and devotion under the guidance of the Holy Spirit.

Psalm 124

Monday
James 5:7-12
Mark 9:38-41

Tuesday
James 5:13-18
Mark 9:42

Wednesday
James 5:19-20
Mark 9:43-48

Thursday
Mark 9:49-50
Esther 1–2

Friday
Esther 3–4
Esther 5–6

Saturday
Esther 7–8
Esther 9–10

Sunday
Esther 7:1-6, 9-10; 9:20-22
Job 1–2

Hymn: "I Want a Principle Within" (UMH 410)

PRAYER Concerns

A Word from John Wesley

Yes, you need to be taught, not only by Mr. Morgan, by one another, by Mr. Maxfield, or me, but by the weakest Preacher in London, yes, by all persons. For God sends to us those whom he will send.

Therefore, do not say to any who would advise or correct you, "You are blind. You cannot teach me." Do not say, "This is your wisdom, your human reason." But calmly discern the thing in the presence of God.

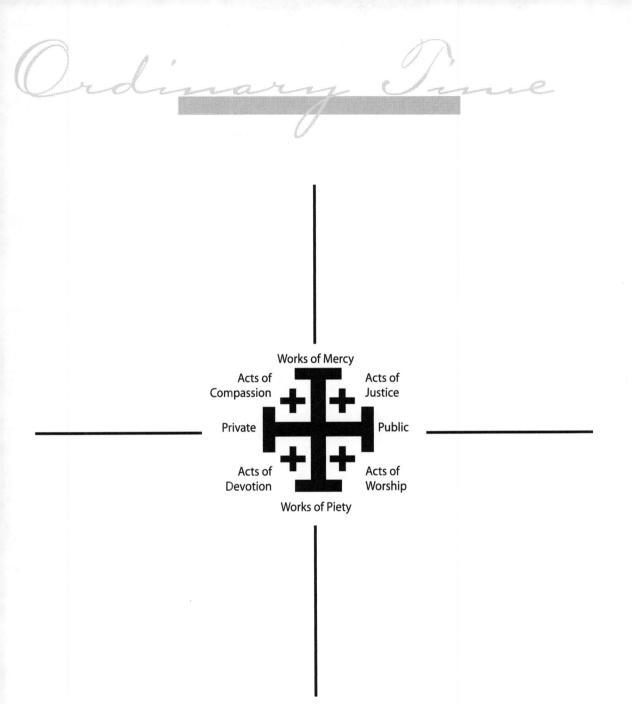

Works of Mercy

Acts of
Compassion

Acts of
Justice

Private

Public

Acts of
Devotion

Acts of
Worship

Works of Piety

To witness to Jesus Christ in the world and to follow his teachings
through acts of compassion, justice, worship, and devotion under the guidance of the Holy Spirit.

Psalm 26

Monday
Job 3
Mark 10:1-12

Tuesday
Job 4–5
Mark 10:13-16

Wednesday
Job 6–7
Hebrews 1

Thursday
Job 8
Hebrews 2

Friday
Job 9–10
Job 11

Saturday
Job 12
Job 13

Sunday
Job 14
Job 15

Hymn: "Blest Be the Dear Uniting Love" (UMH 566)

PRAYER Concerns

A Word from John Wesley

Always remember much grace does not imply much light. These do not always go together. As there may be much light where there is but little love, so there may be much love where there is little light. The heart has more heat than the eye and yet it cannot see. God has wisely assembled the members of the body together such that none may say to another, "I have no need of you."

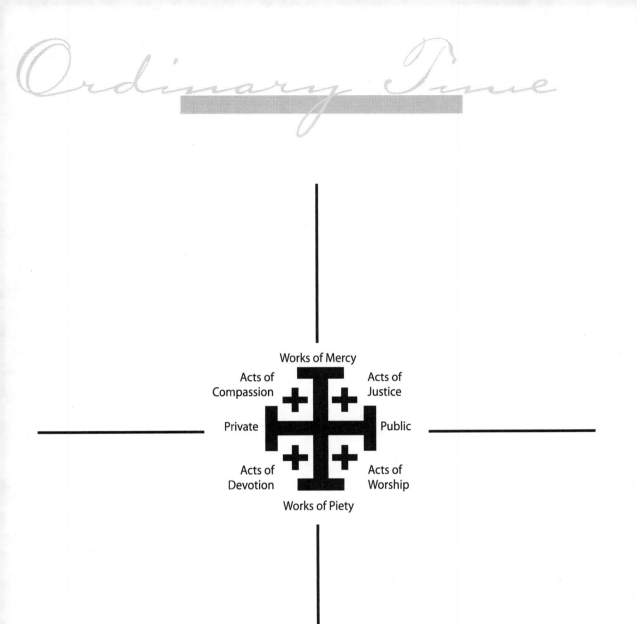

Works of Mercy

Acts of Compassion

Acts of Justice

Private

Public

Acts of Devotion

Acts of Worship

Works of Piety

To witness to Jesus Christ in the world and to follow his teachings
through acts of compassion, justice, worship, and devotion under the guidance of the Holy Spirit.

Psalm 22:1-15

Monday
Job 16-17
Mark 10:17-31

Tuesday
Job 18
Hebrews 3

Wednesday
Job 19
Hebrews 4

Thursday
Job 20
Job 21

Friday
Job 22
Job 23–24

Saturday
Job 25
Job 26

Sunday
Job 27
Job 28

Hymn: "Trust and Obey" (UMH 467)

PRAYER
Concerns

A Word from John Wesley

To imagine none can teach you but those who are themselves saved from sin is a very great and dangerous mistake. Do not entertain it for a moment. It would lead you into a thousand other mistakes from which you may never recover. No, supremacy is not founded in grace, as the madmen of the last age talked. Obey and respect "those who have charge of you in the Lord," and do not think you know better than they. Know their place and your own. Always remember that much love does not imply much light.

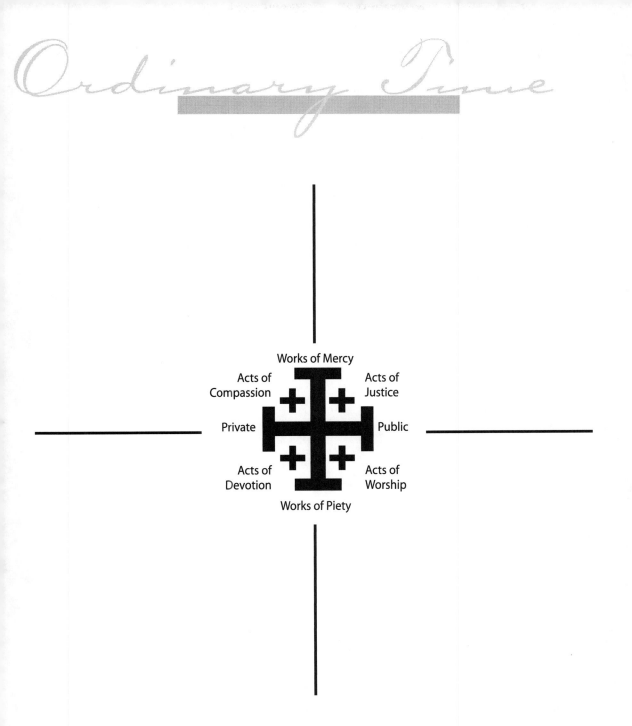

Works of Mercy

Acts of
Compassion

Acts of
Justice

Private

Public

Acts of
Devotion

Acts of
Worship

Works of Piety

To witness to Jesus Christ in the world and to follow his teachings
through acts of compassion, justice, worship, and devotion under the guidance of the Holy Spirit.

Psalm 104:1-9, 24, 35c

Monday
Job 29–30
Mark 10:32-34

Tuesday
Job 31
Mark 10:35-45

Wednesday
Job 32
Hebrews 5:1-10

Thursday
Job 33
Hebrews 5:11-14

Friday
Job 34
Job 35

Saturday
Job 36
Job 37

Sunday
Job 38
Job 39

Hymn: "Jesus, Thine All-Victorious Love" (UMH 422)

PRAYER Concerns

A Word from John Wesley

Q. What is the second advice you would give them?

A. Beware of that child of pride, enthusiasm. Have nothing to do with it! Leave no room for an undisciplined imagination. Do not hastily attribute things to God. Do not easily believe that dreams, voices, impressions, visions, or revelations are from God. They may be from him. They may be from nature. They may be from the devil. Therefore, "do not believe every spirit, but test the spirits to see whether they are from God."

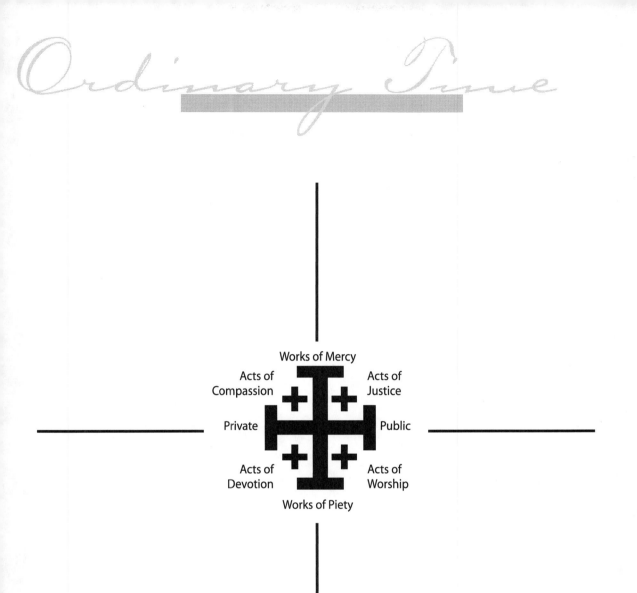

Works of Mercy

Acts of
Compassion

Acts of
Justice

Private

Public

Acts of
Devotion

Acts of
Worship

Works of Piety

To witness to Jesus Christ in the world and to follow his teachings
through acts of compassion, justice, worship, and devotion under the guidance of the Holy Spirit.

Psalm 34:1-8, 19-22

Monday
  Job 40
  Mark 10:46-52

Tuesday
  Job 41
  Hebrews 6:1-12

Wednesday
  Job 42
  Hebrews 6:13-20

Thursday
  Hebrews 7:1-10
  Hebrews 7:11-22

Friday
  Hebrews 7:23-28
  Mark 11:1-11

Saturday
  Hebrews 8:1-6
  Mark 11:12-14, 20-24

Sunday
  Mark 11:15-19
  Mark 11 25-26

Hymn: "Let Us Plead for Faith Alone" (UMH 385)

PRAYER Concerns

A Word from John Wesley

I advise you to never use the words wisdom, reason, or knowledge by way of rebuke. On the contrary, pray that you yourself may abound in them more and more. If you mean worldly wisdom, useless knowledge, or false reasoning, then say so. Throw away the chaff, but not the wheat.

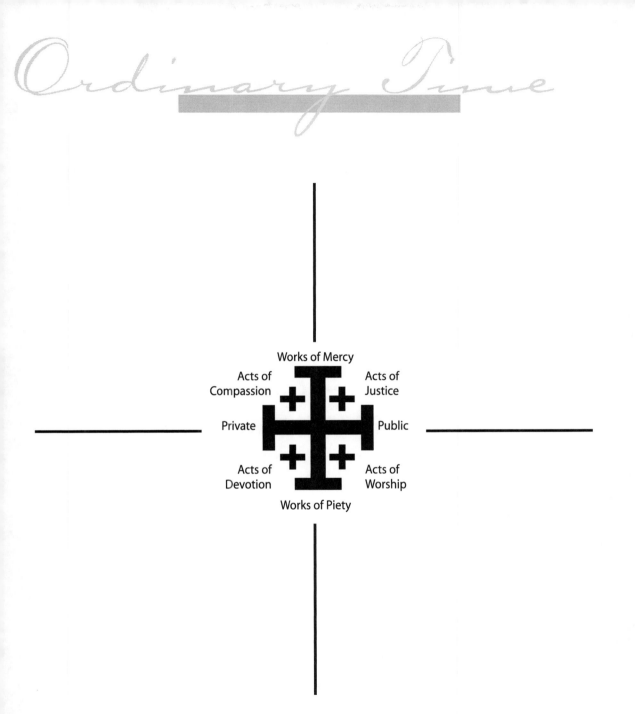

To witness to Jesus Christ in the world and to follow his teachings
through acts of compassion, justice, worship, and devotion under the guidance of the Holy Spirit.

Psalm 146

Hymn: "Where Charity and Love Prevail" (UMH 549)

Monday
Hebrews 8:7-13
Mark 11:27-33

Tuesday
Hebrews 9:1-14
Mark 12:1-12

Wednesday
Hebrews 9:15-22
Mark 12:13-17

Thursday
Ruth 1:1-18
Mark 12:18-27

Friday
Ruth 1:19-22
Mark 12:28-34

Saturday
Hebrews 9:11-14
Mark 12:35-37

Sunday
Mark 12:28-34
Ruth 2:1-13

PRAYER Concerns

A Word from John Wesley

One general entrance to enthusiasm is, expecting the end without the means. For example:

- Expecting knowledge without searching the Scriptures and consulting the children of God.
- Expecting spiritual strength without constant prayer and steady watchfulness.
- Expecting any blessing without hearing the word of God at every opportunity.

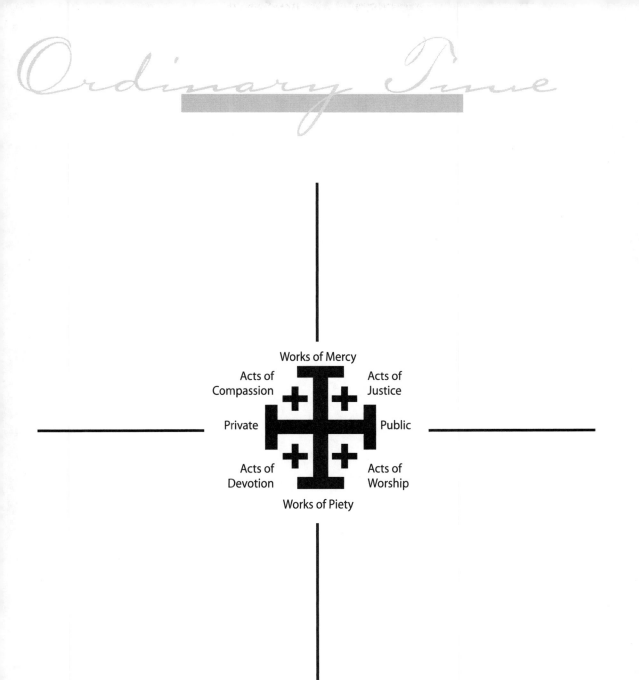

Works of Mercy

Acts of
Compassion

Acts of
Justice

Private

Public

Acts of
Devotion

Acts of
Worship

Works of Piety

To witness to Jesus Christ in the world and to follow his teachings
through acts of compassion, justice, worship, and devotion under the guidance of the Holy Spirit.

Psalm 127

Monday
Ruth 2:14-23
Mark 12:35-37

Tuesday
Ruth 3:1-13
Mark 12:38-40

Wednesday
Ruth 3:14-18
Mark 12:41-44

Thursday
Ruth 4:1-12
Hebrews 9:15-22

Friday
Ruth 4:13-22
Hebrews 9:23-28

Saturday
Ecclesiastes 1
Hebrews 10:1-10

Sunday
Ecclesiastes 2
1 Samuel 1:1-20

Hymn: "A Charge to Keep I Have" (UMH 413)

Prayer Concerns

A Word from John Wesley

It is very important that you thoroughly understand this—"the heaven of heavens is love." There is nothing higher in religion. There is, in effect, nothing else. If you look for anything but more love, you are looking wide of the mark, you are getting out of the royal way. And when you are asking others, "Have you received this or that blessing?" if you mean anything but more love, you mean wrong. You are leading them out of the way, and putting them upon a false path. Settle it then in your heart that from the moment God has saved you from all sin you are to strive for nothing more than more of the love described in 1 Corinthians 13. You can go no higher than this until you are carried into Abraham's bosom.

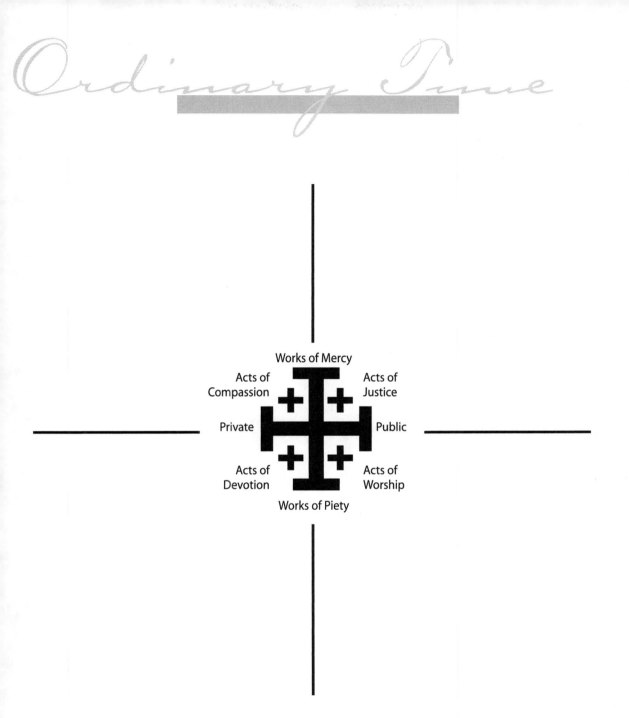

Works of Mercy

Acts of Compassion

Acts of Justice

Private

Public

Acts of Devotion

Acts of Worship

Works of Piety

To witness to Jesus Christ in the world and to follow his teachings
through acts of compassion, justice, worship, and devotion under the guidance of the Holy Spirit.

Psalter: 1 Samuel 2:1-10

Hymn: "Stand By Me" (UMH 512)

Monday
Ecclesiastes 3
1 Samuel 1:21-28

Tuesday
Ecclesiastes 4
Hebrews 10:11-25

Wednesday
Ecclesiastes 5
Hebrews 10:26-39

Thursday
Ecclesiastes 6
Mark 13:1-13

Friday
Ecclesiastes 7
Mark 13:14-23

Saturday
Ecclesiastes 8
Hebrews 11:1-3

Sunday
Ecclesiastes 9
Hebrews 11:4-22

PRAYER Concerns

A Word from John Wesley

Beware of Antinomianism, or "canceling out any part of the law through faith." Enthusiasm naturally leads to this. Indeed they can hardly be separated . . .

Beware of thinking, "Because I am filled with love, I don't need to have so much holiness. Because I pray always, I don't need a set time for private prayer. Because I am always mindful of my behavior, I don't need personal self-examination." Let us "magnify the law," the whole written word, "and make it honorable." Let this be our proclamation: "I prize your commandments above gold or precious stones. O what love I have for your law! I study in it all day long."

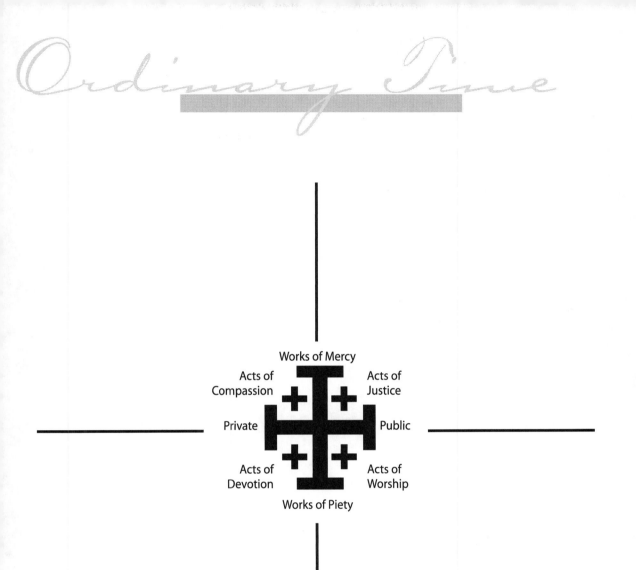

Works of Mercy

Acts of
Compassion

Acts of
Justice

Private

Public

Acts of
Devotion

Acts of
Worship

Works of Piety

To witness to Jesus Christ in the world and to follow his teachings
through acts of compassion, justice, worship, and devotion under the guidance of the Holy Spirit.

LEADING TO CHRIST THE KING / REIGN OF CHRIST
(Sunday between November 20 and 26)

Psalm 132:1-12

Monday
2 Samuel 23:1-7
Hebrews 11:23-40

Tuesday
Ecclesiastes 10
Revelation 1:4b-8

Wednesday
Ecclesiastes 11
John 18:33-37

Thursday
Ecclesiastes 12
Joel 2:21-27*

Friday
1 Timothy 2:1-7*
Matthew 6:25-33*
Psalm 126*

Saturday
Hebrews 12:1-13
Hebrews 12:14-29

Sunday
Hebrews 13:1-17
Hebrews 13:18-25

*Thanksgiving Readings

Hymn: "Rejoice, the Lord Is King" (UMH 715)

PRAYER Concerns

A Word from John Wesley

Beware of desiring anything but God. Now you desire nothing else; every other desire is driven out. See that none enter again. "Keep thyself pure;" let your "eye" remain "healthy, and your whole body shall be full of light." Allow no desire of pleasing food, or any other pleasure of sense. Allow no desire of pleasing the eye or the imagination by anything grand, or new, or beautiful. Allow no desire of money, of praise, or esteem. Do not desire happiness in any creature. You may bring these desires back, but you need not. You need feel them no more. Stand firm in the liberty with which Christ has made you free.

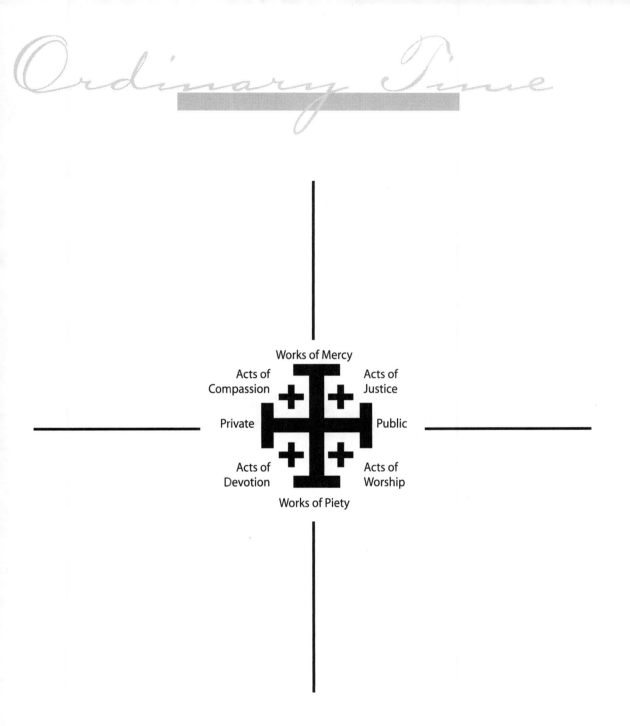

Works of Mercy

Acts of Compassion

Acts of Justice

Private

Public

Acts of Devotion

Acts of Worship

Works of Piety

To witness to Jesus Christ in the world and to follow his teachings
through acts of compassion, justice, worship, and devotion under the guidance of the Holy Spirit.

An Order for Devotion

In the Morning

Call to Prayer (from Psalm 51)

> Open my lips, O Lord,
>> and my mouth shall proclaim your praise.
>
> Create in me a clean heart, O God,
>> and renew a right spirit within me.
>
> Cast me not away from your presence
>> and take not your Holy Spirit from me.
>
> Give me the joy of your saving help again
>> and sustain me with your bountiful Spirit.
>
> Glory to the Father, and to the Son, and to the Holy Spirit:
>> as it was in the beginning, is now, and will be for ever. Amen.

Scripture: The Psalm and one of the lessons for the day are read.

Silence

Hymn: The hymn for the week may be used; the Apostles' Creed may be said.

Prayers for Ourselves and for Others

The Lord's Prayer

The Collect: See Collects for the Evening on the reverse side, or pray the following:

> Lord God, almighty and everlasting Father,
>> you have brought us in safety to this new day:
>
> Preserve us with your mighty power,
>> that we may not fall into sin,
>> nor be overcome by adversity;
>
> and in all we do, direct us to the fulfilling of your purpose;
> through Jesus Christ our Lord. Amen.

In the Evening

Call to Prayer

> O gracious Light,
>> pure brightness of the everliving Father in heaven,
>
> O Jesus Christ, holy and blessed!
>
> Now as we come to the setting of the sun,
>> and our eyes behold the evening light,
>> we sing your praises, O God: Father, Son, and Holy Spirit.
>
> You are worthy at all times to be praised by happy voices,
>> O Son of God, O Giver of life,
>
> and to be glorified through all the worlds.

Scripture: One of the lessons for the day may be read.

Silence

Hymn: The hymn for the week may be used; the Apostles' Creed may be said.

Prayers for Ourselves and for Others

The Lord's Prayer

The Collect: See Collects for the Evening on the reverse side, or pray the following:

> The collect for the day of the week or for the season or the following may be said:
>
> Lord Jesus, stay with us,
>> for evening is at hand and the day is past;
>> be our companion in the way,
>
> kindle out hearts, and awaken hope,
>> that we may know you as you are revealed in Scripture
>> and the breaking of bread.
>
> Grant this for the sake of your love. Amen.